SACRED WORDS

*A Selection of Spiritual
Writings of All Ages*

This compilation copyright © Paul Ladouceur 1996 and
individual copyright holders (see list on pages 258–260)

First published 1996

ISBN 1 – 899171 – 65 – 7

British Library Cataloguing-in-Publication Data
A catalogue record for this book is available from the British Library

Set in Times New Roman by Posthouse Printing and Publishing Ltd
Printed and bound by Interprint Ltd., Malta

Published by
Findhorn Press
The Park, Findhorn,
Forres IV36 0TZ, Scotland.
+44 (0)1309-690582 / fax 690036
e-mail thierry@findhorn.org
http://www.mcn.org/findhorn/press/   *or*
http://www.gaia.org/findhornpress/

SACRED WORDS

A Selection of Spiritual
Writings of All Ages

Edited and Compiled by
Paul Ladouceur

FINDHORN
Press

FOR SAVANNAH, KARIM AND ALEX

With special appreciation to Aileen McKenna
who first showed me the path

TABLE OF CONTENTS

Let him who seeks
continue seeking until he finds.
When he finds, he will become troubled.
When he becomes troubled, he will be astonished,
and he will rule over the all.

The Gospel of Thomas

The dust of ignorance has been since of old
accumulating on the mirror never polished.
Now is the time once for all to see
the clearing positively done.

Yoka Daishi, *Shodoka*

One should not rely on
the person of a teacher,
but on his teachings.

Mahayana-Sutra-Lankara

PREFACE

The sacred writings of humanity constitute its greatest written treasures. They provide a vision of the divine, a gateway to God, and invite all those who read and reflect on them to open their hearts and their minds to their innermost selves, to their highest aspirations, to the divinity itself. They are humanity's spiritual nourishment. For God has revealed himself throughout the ages to men and women the world over, and the personal and collective experience of God is contained in sacred texts going back to the earliest known writings.

This collection presents a selection of major sacred writings of the world's principal religious and spiritual traditions. Both traditional and more recent texts are included. Why such a wide spectrum of writings from different traditions, teachers and ages? Without affirming that in effect all religions and spiritual traditions are the same, we can assert with Sri Ramakrishna that all religions are paths which lead to God - but the paths are not God. Each of us must find and follow his or her own spiritual path, but we can find nourishment and inspiration from the wisdom of the sacred writings of all traditions. Many are those who have preceded us to the divine and many are the paths they have followed.

It is for this reason that we have adopted a liberal definition of what constitutes a "sacred text". If writings such as the Bible, the Bhagavad Gita, the Koran and many of the Buddhist sutras can easily be admitted as "sacred texts", this is less obvious for many of the other choices included in this collection. Nonetheless, the wisdom, beauty and relevance of the words of many great spiritual teachers of the past and present are also valuable spiritual nourishment for our own time.

This collection has been prepared with two thoughts in mind. First, it provides a sample of significant sacred writings for those whose exposure to such works may be limited, and who wish to explore beyond their previous experience and knowledge.

Secondly, the texts offer a basis for personal reflection; each has sufficient substance – generally one or two pages – to constitute material for reflection, meditation and discussion. These writings are not mere museum pieces, beautiful in themselves and certainly deserving of our admiration – but cut off from our personal and inner lives; rather, they should be seen as living messages which speak to every one of us. As a further aid towards personal reflection and experience of the texts, a few phrases or sentences, based on the principal document, are included at the end of each. These are not summaries or abstracts of the texts, but are personal reflections or meditations to assist in making the text more meaningful to the reader – an invitation to the reader to do likewise.

Other than the short meditation, based directly on the text itself, no introductions or commentaries are provided on the documents: they are allowed to speak for themselves. Although our understanding of many of these texts in often greatly enhanced by inspired commentaries and interpretations, this is not the role or place of this particular book. Major religious writings such as the Vedas, the Bible, the Koran and the Sutras have been the subject of important commentaries over the centuries and in fact many of these commentaries are themselves significant religious documents. The reader may wish to gain a deeper knowledge of the writings by consulting the full works cited in the Bibliography.

Very few of these texts were originally written in European languages; many, in fact, were written in languages which have long since fallen out of current use: Sanskrit, Pali, classical Greek, historical Hebrew, Latin etc. Other texts were originally written in languages whose translation into modern European languages is often difficult: classical Persian, Mandarin Chinese, and Tibetan, for example. Every effort has been made to identify the most literary and meaningful translation of a particular text selected for this volume, and in a few cases, original adaptations based on several versions have been prepared. Some translators occasionally prefer to retain certain original words, particularly for Buddhist and Hindu writings, since there are no accurate corresponding words in English. In some cases, acceptable translations of certain words have been added in brackets or substituted for the original words, and as a further aid in understanding oriental texts, a glossary of terms commonly used in Buddhist, Hindu and Taoist writings is provided.

Such a collection of extracts of sacred writings reflects the personal choices of the editor. In addition to the wish to have a broadly representative selection of the world's sacred writings, I have chosen works which reflect important aspects of the philosophical and theological teachings of the major spiritual traditions. The texts emphasize speculations on the nature of the divine and the finality of human existence, their implications for the individual, and knowledge of God and spiritual experience, rather than religious practices, ritual and ethical codes.

"God created man in his image" (*Genesis* 1, 27): we as humans reflect God in our being and his becoming: in our being, as living, spiritual beings. In our becoming, because this divine image is hidden behind the "mask of gold" (*Isa Upanishad*) of the visible world; the becoming of humankind is to discover and to realize our divine nature, our Christ nature, our Buddha nature. Thus, when we say that God is love, light, joy, wisdom, as well as silence and mystery, these are also our own nature, in our being and our becoming. The writings included here speak of these qualities not only as qualities of the divine, but also as qualities, potential and experience of humankind, created in the divine image.

The broad themes under which the texts are grouped are admittedly somewhat arbitrary, since many writings cover several topics simultaneously. Texts in each section display similarities of thought, experience and aspiration across different spiritual traditions. To assist in identifying the origins of the various writings, a table at the end of the book groups them according to spiritual traditions.

Can one legitimately include Buddhist texts under headings which refer directly to "God"? A difficult question to the extent that Buddhism has no specific notion of "God", as in other spiritual traditions. Yet Buddhism is unquestionably among the great spiritualities of humanity which, despite the absence of a precise concept of "God", nonetheless deals with the spiritual realm, the "beyond", the transcendental, "emptiness" or "void" (*shunyata*) in Buddhist terminology. In this, Buddhism has a great deal in common with the other major traditions, as much as in its philosophy of humankind and the means to achieve realization of the true self and the transcendental.

One cannot but have a great sense of awe and humility before the timeless wisdom and beauty of the world's sacred writings. I hope that those who read and use this selection will also feel the wisdom and beauty of the writings and, through them, will grow in the knowledge and love of the divine – in themselves, in others and in the universe.

*   *   *

This book was prepared simultaneously in both English and French versions, and I wish to express many profound appreciations to all those who gave their assistance, in particular Anne-Marie de Brabandère for the French version, and Jancis Browning for the English version. Their encouragement and collaboration were very important.

I also wish to thank the authors, translators and publishers of the writings from which extracts are included in this book.

Paul Ladouceur
Archamps, France
January 1996

1 GOD IS THE UNIQUE

THE WORD OF GOD

IN the beginning was the Word,
 and the Word was with God,
    and the Word was God.
He was in the beginning with God.
All things came into being through him,
    and without him not one thing came into being.
What has come into being in him was life,
    and the life was the light of all people.
The light shines in the darkness,
    and the darkness did not overcome it.

There was a man sent from God, whose name was John. He came
as a witness to testify to the light, so that all might believe through
him. He himself was not the light, but he came to testify to the light.

The true light,
    which enlightens everyone,
    was coming into the world.
He was in the world,
    and the world came into being through him;
    yet the world did not know him.
He came to what was his own,
    and his own people did not accept him.

But to all who received him, who believed in his name, he gave
power to become children of God, who were born, not of blood or
of the will of the flesh nor of the will of man, but of God.

And the Word became flesh
  and lived among us,
  and we have seen his glory,
  the glory as of the Father's only Son,
  full of grace and truth.

John testified to him and cried out, "This was he of whom I said, 'He who comes after me ranks ahead of me because he was before me.'" From his fullness we have all received, grace upon grace. The law indeed was given through Moses; grace and truth came through Jesus Christ. No one has ever seen God. It is God the only Son, who is close to the Father's heart, who has made him known.

The Gospel According to John, 1

In the beginning was the Word:
the Word was God,
the light and life of the world,
who lived among us.

THE ETERNAL WAY

THE WAY that can be told
Is not the eternal Way;
The name that can be named
Is not the unchanging Name.

The nameless is the origin of heaven and earth;
The named is the mother of all creatures.
Hence always be without desires
  in order to observe its subtleties;
And always have desires
  in order to observe its manifestations.

These two are the same
But have different names as they are manifested.
Because they are the same, they are called mysteries:
Mystery of mysteries, the gateway of all secrets.

There is a thing undefined yet complete,
Existent before heaven and earth.
Silent and formless,
Standing alone and unchanging,
Present everywhere and never exhausted,
It is thought of as the mother of the universe.
I know not its name,
So I call it the Way.
Pressed further, I call it Great;
Greatness signifies acting everywhere;
Acting everywhere signifies reaching far away;
Reaching far away signifies returning to the beginning.

Lao Tzu, *Tao Te Ching*, I and XXV

> *The Way is beyond words and names:*
> *the beginning and the end of all,*
> *complete, eternal, unchanging.*

BEHIND THE CIRCLE OF GOLD

BEHOLD the universe in the glory of God: and all that lives and moves on earth. Leaving the transient, find joy in the Eternal: set not your heart on another's possession.

Working thus, a man may wish for a life of a hundred years. Only actions done in God bind not the soul of man.

There are demon-haunted worlds, regions of utter darkness. Whoever in life denies the Spirit falls into that darkness of death.

The Spirit, without moving, is swifter than the mind; the senses cannot reach him; He is ever beyond them. Standing still, he over-takes those who run. To the ocean of his being, the spirit of life leads the streams of action.

He moves, and he moves not. He is far, and he is near. He is within all, and he is outside all. Who sees all beings in his own self, and his own self in all beings, loses all fear.

When a sage sees this great unity and his self has become all beings, what delusion and what sorrow can ever be near him?

The Spirit filled all with his radiance. He is incorporeal and invulnerable, pure and untouched by evil. He is the supreme seer and thinker, immanent and transcendent. He placed all things in the path of eternity.

Into deep darkness fall those who follow action. Into deeper darkness fall those who follow knowledge. One is the outcome of knowledge, and another is the outcome of action. Thus have we heard from the ancient sages who explained this truth to us.

He who knows both knowledge and action, with action overcomes death and with knowledge reaches immortality.

Into deep darkness fall those who follow the immanent. Into deeper darkness fall those who follow the transcendent. One is the outcome of the transcendent, and another is the outcome of the immanent. Thus have we heard from the ancient sages who explained this truth to us.

He who knows both the transcendent and the immanent, with the immanent overcomes death and with the transcendent reaches immortality.

The face of truth remains hidden behind a circle of gold. Unveil it, O god of light, that I who love the true may see!

O life-giving sun, offspring of the Lord of creation, solitary seer of heaven! Spread thy light and withdraw thy blinding splendour that I may behold thy radiant form: that Spirit far away within thee is my own inmost Spirit.

May life go to immortal life, and the body go to ashes. OM. O my soul, remember past strivings, remember! By the path of good lead us to final bliss, O fire divine, thou god who knowest all ways. Deliver us from wandering evil. Prayers and adoration we offer unto thee.

Isa Upanishad

That which is, is distant;
that which is, is near;
behind the circle of gold
shines the light of eternal truth.

THE ONE MIND

ALL the Buddhas and all sentient beings are nothing but the One Mind, beside which nothing exists. This Mind, which is without beginning, is unborn and indestructible. It is not green nor yellow, and has neither form nor appearance. It does not belong to the categories of things that exist or do not exist, nor can it be thought of in terms of new or old. It is neither long nor short, big nor small, for it transcends all limits, measures, names, traces, and comparisons. It is that which you see before you – begin to reason about it and you at once fall into error. It is like the boundless void which cannot be fathomed or measured.

The One Mind alone is the Buddha and there is no distinction between the Buddha and sentient beings, but that sentient beings are attached to forms and so seek externally for Buddhahood. By their very seeking they lose it, for that is using the Buddha to seek for the Buddha and using mind to grasp Mind. Even though they do their utmost for a full aeon, they will not be able to attain it. They do not know that, if they put a stop to conceptual thought and forget their anxiety, the Buddha will appear before them, for this Mind is the Buddha and the Buddha is all living beings...

As to performing the six *paramitas* and vast numbers of similar practices, or gaining merits as countless as the sands of the Ganges, since you are fundamentally complete in every respect, you should not try to supplement that perfection by such meaningless practices. When there is occasion for them, perform them, and when the occasion is passed, remain quiescent. If you are not absolutely convinced that the Mind is the Buddha, and if you are attached to forms, practices and meritorious performances, your way of thinking is false and quite incompatible with the Way. The Mind is the Buddha, nor are there other Buddhas or any other mind. It is bright and spotless as the void, having no form or appearance whatever. To make use of your minds to think conceptually is to leave the substance and attach yourselves to form. The Ever-existent Buddha is not a Buddha of form or attachment. [...]

Our original Buddha-nature is, in highest truth, devoid of any atom of objectivity. It is void, omnipresent, silent, pure; it is glorious and mysterious peaceful joy – and that is all. Enter deeply in it by awakening to it yourself. That which is before you is it, in all its fullness, utterly complete. There is naught beside. Even if you go through all the stages of a bodhisattva's progress towards Buddhahood, one by one – when at last, in a single flash, you attain to full realization, you will only be realizing the Buddha-nature which has been with you all the time; and by all the foregoing stages you will have added to it nothing at all. You will come to look upon those aeons of work and achievement as no better than unreal actions performed in a dream. That is why the Tathagata said: "I truly attained nothing from complete, unexcelled enlightenment."

The Teachings of Huang Po, *On the Transmission of Mind*, 1-3

The One Mind is the Buddha;
the Buddha is the One Mind;
all which lives partakes of the One Mind:
we are all Buddha.

YOU ARE ALL NAMES AND NONE

YOU are above all things
   and what other way
   can we rightly sing of you?
How can words sing your praise
   when no word can speak of you?
How can the mind consider you
   when no mind can ever grasp you?
You alone are unutterable
   from the time you created
   all things that can be spoken of.
You alone are unknowable
   from the time you created
   all things that can be known.

All things cry out about you,
   those which speak,
   and those which cannot speak.
All things honour you,
   those which think,
   and those which cannot think.
For there is one longing, one groaning,
   that all things have for you.

All things pray to you
   that comprehend your plan
   and offer you a silent hymn.
In you, the One, all things abide
   and all things endlessly run to you
   who are the end of all.
And you are the One, and All,
   and none of them -
   being not one thing, not all things.

You who bear all names,
   how shall I name you,
   who cannot be named?

What heavenly mind can penetrate
  those veils above the clouds?
Be merciful,
  you who are greater than all things,
  for what other way
  can we rightly sing of you?

Gregory of Nazianzen, "Hymn to God"

How can I rightly render homage to you
  who are all names,
  who are above names,
  who are honoured by all creation?

CREATION HYMN

THERE was neither non-existence nor existence then; there was neither the realm of space nor the sky which is beyond. What stirred? Where? In whose protection? Was there water, bottomlessly deep?

There was neither death nor immortality then. There was no distinguishing sign of night or day. That one breathed, windless, by its own impulse. Other than that there was nothing beyond.

Darkness was hidden by darkness in the beginning; with no distinguishing sign, all this was water. The life force that was covered with emptiness, that one arose through the power of heat.

Desire came upon that one in the beginning: that was the first seed of mind. Poets seeking in their heart with wisdom found the bond of existence in non-existence.

The cord was extended across. Was there below? Was there above? There were seed-placers; there were powers. There was impulse beneath; there was giving-forth above.

Who really knows? Who will here proclaim it? Whence was it produced? Whence is this creation? The gods came afterwards, with the creation of this universe. Who then knows whence it has arisen?

Whence this creation has arisen – perhaps it formed itself, or perhaps it did not – the one who looks down upon it, in the highest heaven, only he knows – or perhaps he does not know.

Rig Veda, 10.129 (*Nasadiya*)

Whence is this universe,
the visible and the invisible?
Where was I before the universe?
Only the One that is, knows.

HE IS HERE

I WAS on that day when the names were not,
Nor any sign of existence endowed with name.
By me names and named were brought to view
On the day when there were not "I" and "we".
For a sign, the tip of the Beloved's curl
 became a centre of revelation;
As yet the tip of that fair curl was not.

Cross and Christians, from end to end,
I surveyed; he was not on the cross.
I went to the idol-temple, to the ancient pagoda;
No trace was visible there.
I went to the mountains of Herat and Candahar;
I looked; he was not in that hill-and-dale.

With set purpose I fared to the summit of Mount Qaf;
In that place was only the 'Anqa's habitation.
I bent the reins of search to the Ka'ba;
He was not in that resort of old and young.
I questioned Ibn Sina of his state;
He was not in Ibn Sina's range.
I fared towards the scene
    of *two bow-lengths' distance* (*Koran*, 53);
He was not in that exalted court.

I gazed into my own heart;
There I saw him; he was nowhere else.

Jalal od-Din Rumi, Divan-i-Shams-i-Tabriz

> *Where is he, who was before names were?*
> *He is neither here, nor there,*
> *but only within the depths of my heart.*

BEING AND THE ONE

THE NAME of "being" is rightly applied by theology to him who truly is... The purpose of what I have to say is not to reveal that being in its transcendence, for this is something beyond words, something unknown and wholly unrevealed, something above unity itself. What I wish to do is to sing a hymn of praise for the being-making procession of the absolute divine Source of being into the total domain of being. [...]

The God who is transcends everything by virtue of his power. He is the substantive cause and maker of being, subsistence, of existence, of substance, and of nature. He is the source and the measure of the ages. He is the reality beneath time and the eternity behind being. He is the time within which things happen. He is being for whatever is. He is coming-to-be amid whatever happens. From him who is come eternity, essence and being, come time, genesis, and becoming. He is the being immanent in and underlying the things which are, however they are. For God is not some kind of being. No. But in a way that is simple and indefinable he gathers into himself and anticipates every existence. So he is called "King of the ages" (1 *Timothy* 1), for in him and around him all being is and subsists. He was not. He will not be. He did not come to be. He is not in the midst of becoming. He will not come to be. No. He is not. Rather, he is the essence of being for the things which have being. Not only things that are but also the essence of what they are come from him who precedes the ages. For he is the age of ages, the "predecessor of the ages" (*Psalm* 55).

To repeat. Every being and all the ages derive their existence from the Preexistent. All eternity and time are from him. The Preexistent is the source and is the cause of all eternity, of time and of every kind of being. Everything participates in him and none among beings falls away. "He himself is before all things, and in him all things hold together" (*Colossians*, 1). In short, the existence of anything whatsoever is there in the Preexistent, and is perceived and preserved.

Being precedes the entities which participate in it. Being in itself is more revered than the being of life itself and wisdom itself and likeness to divinity itself. Whatever beings participate in these things must, before all else, participate in being. More precisely, those absolute qualities of which things have a share must themselves participate in being itself. Consider anything which is. Its being and eternity is Being itself. So therefore God as originator of everything through the first of all his gifts is praised as "He who is" (*Exodus* 3). [...]

The name "One" means that God is uniquely all things through the transcendence of one unity and that he is the cause of all without ever departing from that oneness. Nothing in the world lacks its share of the One. Just as every number participates in unity..., so everything, and every part of everything, participates in the One. By being the One, it is in all things. The One cause of all things is not one of the many things in the world but actually precedes oneness and multiplicity and indeed defines oneness and multiplicity. For multiplicity cannot exist without some participation in the One. That which is many in its parts is one in its entirety. That which is many in its accidental qualities is one in its subject. That which is many in number or capabilities is one in species. That which is numerous in species is one in genus. That which is numerous in its processions is one in its source. For there is nothing at all lacking a share in that One which in its utterly comprehensive unity uniquely contains all and every thing beforehand, even opposites. Without the One there is no multiplicity, but there can still be the One when there is no multiplicity, just as one precedes all multiplied number. And, then, if one thinks of all things as united in all things, the totality of things must be presumed to be one.

Pseudo-Dionysius, *The Divine Names*, 5-6

---

*God is the transcendent and pre-existent One
from whom all being flows,
from whom time flows;
all creation participates in his Oneness.*

THE PERSONAL AND IMPERSONAL

WHEN the Supreme Being is thought of as inactive – neither creating, sustaining nor destroying – I call him by the name *Brahman* or
Purusha (the male principle), the Impersonal God. When I think of
him as active – creating, sustaining, destroying – I call him by the
name of *Shakti* or *Maya* or *Prakriti* (the female principle), or the
Personal God... But in fact the distinction between Brahman, the
inactive or Impersonal God on the one hand, and Shakti, the active
or Personal God on the other, is a distinction without a difference.
The Impersonal and the Personal are one and the same being, even
as fire and its burning property are one. You cannot conceive of fire
apart from its power of burning, nor the power of burning apart from
the fire. They are one, even as milk and its whiteness are one. One
cannot conceive of milk without the whiteness. [...]

My Holy Mother is none other than the Absolute. She it is to
whom the six systems of philosophy with all their learned disquisi-
tions furnish no clue.

When the differentiated ego is taken away by my Mother, there
comes the realisation of the Impersonal in samadhi, and then it is the
Impersonal God, not the individual soul, that realises the
Impersonal. When the ego is purified and so retained, the seeing or
realisation of the Personal God or any of her manifestations is possible by her grace – manifestations such as Sri Krishna, Chaitanya
Deva and other divine incarnations... It pleases my Mother, the
Personal God, to efface the self in selfless samadhi. The result is the
realisation of the Impersonal God in samadhi. Sometimes it pleases
her to keep that self on in her devotees and then to appear before
them as the Personal God, and talk with them. The key to the realisation of the Absolute is with the Divine Person alone, the *Saguna
Brahman* of the Upanishads, the Personal God of devotees... The
Divine Person, my Holy Mother, is the Personal side of the one reality, the Absolute (the Brahman of the Vedanta). Yes, my Mother herself has declared to her children, "I am", "I am the mother of the
universe", "I am the Brahman of the Vedanta", "I am the Atman of
the Upanishads."

Thus the Personal God reveals herself. That revelation is the
proof of her existence. Again, the Impersonal, Undifferentiated God,

the Absolute, is revealed by the Personal God, that is, the personal side of God the Absolute. The saint in samadhi cannot say anything about the Absolute... Nor can he, coming down from samadhi, say anything about the Absolute. Once differentiated, he is mute as to the Undifferentiated. Once in the relative world his mouth is shut as to the Absolute and Unconditioned. [...]

The manifestation of the Personal God is often a spiritual form which is seen only by the purified human soul. In other words, these forms are realised by the organs of spiritual vision, belonging to that spiritual body which is derived from the Lord. Not every one, but only the perfected man can see these divine forms through the grace of my Mother. [...]

So long as you are a person, an individuality of your own, God will, if it so pleases him, manifest himself to you as a person. Nor can you conceive of, think of, or perceive God otherwise than as a person, so long as you are a person. Such is the constitution of your self.

The goal of the Advaitist [follower of non-dualism] is the merging of the conditioned ego in the Unconditioned Brahman. This is not meant by my Divine Mother for everybody. For the majority of mankind the ego is a thing which cannot be shaken off in this life, or any other life in the near future.

Thus, they must, so long as they cannot attain to samadhi, meditate upon, and commune with, the Personal God. For sages and the scriptures and revelation all agree in assuring us that the Unconditioned does manifest itself to man, both within him and without him, as a conditioned being: the Impersonal as a Personal God. These personal manifestations are by no means less real, but infinitely more real than the body or the mind or the external world. "Hence," says the sage, "the necessity of a Personal God."

The Gospel of Sri Ramakrishna

> *God is the One and the Absolute;*
> *he is not limited by our conception of him:*
> *hence God conceived as Person is one*
> *and the same as God conceived without Person.*

THE ESSENTIAL BEING

INTRINSICALLY, that is to say, in his essence, man is an aspect of Divine Being, whose purpose is to manifest itself in him and through him. Just as flowers and animals in their own way reveal Divine Being, so also must man reveal it in the way of man. He can only be "right" when his life-form, with all its forces, fulfils the destiny that dwells within him as his essential being.

For each of us, our essential being is the medium through which we participate in Divine Being. It may also be said to be the means by which Divine Being strives through us to manifest itself in the world – not as something apart from the world, a mere spiritual inwardness, but as a bodily presence. It follows that our human inner growth is necessarily accomplished within the framework of our worldly destiny, in the midst of ordinary life and the carrying out of daily tasks.

Man's destiny is to bear witness, in his own special way, to Divine Being – which is to say, consciously and freely. Flowers and animals fulfil theirs of necessity and unconsciously, limited only by whatever external conditions may hinder them from becoming what, in their essence, they are. Man, however, unlike flowers and animals, has been endowed with consciousness; and it is by means of this quality that, as an "I", he is able to stand and confront the world. Because of this he becomes, at least to some extent, independent and therefore responsible for his own development. Herein lies his great chance. But here, too, let us not forget, lies danger. For between this chance and this danger he may miss the mark.

The "oneness" of that Life which is beyond space and time breaks apart in man's ego-consciousness into two poles: one, the *historical world* which, being subject to laws of space and time, can be understood and mastered; and two, *Transcendental Being*, which cannot be encompassed by space and time and is beyond all ordinary understanding. Thus, inevitably, man experiences himself as a being standing between heaven and earth. He lives in a state of tension between two realities: the world, which confines him to latitude, longitude and duration, endangers his existence, tempts him with hopes of happiness, and demands his obedience to its laws; and the supernatural state of Being within him and towards which, even unknowingly, he yearns. Ceaselessly striving to find the light, this Being calls him forth beyond the laws and boundaries of his little personal life, to the service of Greater Life. [...]

The purpose of all living things, man among them, is to manifest the Divine in the world. Man's distinctive virtue lies in the fact that the great, the Divine Life becomes in him "conscious of itself". In the freedom of conscious life – as opposed to mechanical life – the Divine can shine forth and take form. Therefore the true man is he who, in freedom and with clear awareness, embodies and reveals the Divine Being within himself. The vividness of his inner life, the radiance of his being and the benign effect of his actions will all give evidence of his inner state. Such a state enables Divine Being in all its plenitude, inner order and unity to appear.

Karlfried Graf Dürckheim, *The Way of Transformation*

> *My essential being is the Divine within me:*
> *my vocation is to bear witness*
> *to the Divine Being,*
> *through the outer visible person.*

OM IS BRAHMAN

OM. This eternal word is all: what was, what is and what shall be, and what beyond is in eternity. All is OM. Brahman is all and Atman is Brahman.

Atman, the Self, has four conditions. The first condition is the waking life of outward-moving consciousness, enjoying the seven outer gross elements.

The second condition is the dreaming life of inner-moving consciousness, enjoying the seven subtle inner elements in its own light and solitude.

The third condition is the sleeping life of silent consciousness when a person has no desires and beholds no dreams. That condition of deep sleep is one of oneness, a mass of silent consciousness made of peace and enjoying peace. This silent consciousness is all-powerful, all-knowing, the inner ruler, the source of all, the beginning and end of all beings.

The fourth condition is Atman in his own pure state: the awakened life of supreme consciousness. It is neither outer nor inner consciousness, neither semi-consciousness nor sleeping consciousness, neither consciousness nor unconsciousness. He is Atman, the spirit himself, that cannot be seen or touched, that is above all distinction, beyond thought and ineffable. In the union with him is the supreme proof of his reality. He is the end of evolution and non-duality. He is peace and love.

This Atman is the eternal word OM. Its three sounds, A, U, and M, are the first three states of consciousness, and these three states are the three sounds. The first sound A is the first state of waking consciousness, common to all men. It is found in the words *apti*, "attaining", and *adimatvam*, "being first". Who knows this attains in truth all his desires, and in all things becomes first.

The second sound U is the second state of dreaming consciousness. It is found in the words *utkarsha*, "uprising", and *ubhayatvam*, "bothness". Who knows this raises the tradition of knowledge and attains equilibrium. In his family is never born anyone who knows not Brahman.

The third sound M is the third state of sleeping consciousness. It is found in the words *miti*, "measure", and in the root *mi*, "to end", that gives *apiti*, "final end". Who knows this measures all with his mind and attains the final End.

The word OM as one sound is the fourth state of supreme consciousness. It is beyond the senses and is the end of evolution. It is non-duality and love. He goes with his self to the supreme Self who knows this, who knows this.

Mandukya Upanishad

> OM: *the eternal word,*
> *the beginning and the end,*
> *which encompasses the totality of human existence,*
> *and unites with the eternal.*

THE GREATNESS OF GOD

In the name of him whose kingdom is unending,
  in describing whom the speech of the wise
  is reduced to dumbness.
His name is a joyous message to the souls of men;
  it appears at the head of the poets' divans.
To think of his name is to cover the palate of the soul with sugar;
  to mention it is to cover the sword of the tongue with jewels.
Scent without mention of his name is but colour;
  fame without mention of his name is downright disgrace.
He is a Lord beside whose being all that has existence
  is the essence of lowness.

Since his being is higher than all we know of,
  how then can we describe it?
With the hand of creation he flung the ball of the terrestrial globe
  into the crook of the polo-stick of the celestial spheres.
Since no man's intellect can rise above him,
  no man can know the extent of his favours.
All negation of the world is affirmation of him;
  the whole universe is proof of his being.

His attributes are his being and his being his attributes:
  if you consider well he is all being.
All that exists is but the shadow of his presence;
  it is all the effect of his omnipotent creation.
An eloquent speaker said well of his being
  that the belief in God's unity springs from the rejection
  of all accessories.
So lofty is his rank, that everything from the moon
  to the fish is to his eye as black as hair.
So great are his glory and his self-sufficiency,
  that all the minds and souls of men are but
  so many playthings to him.
Such is his majesty that were it to enter a man's soul
  a hundred storms would spring up in every atom.
Such is his unity that it does not leave room for a single hair;

beside his unity the whole world does not weigh a single hair.
Such is his mercy that did Iblis [Satan] receive
 the smallest portion of it
 he would bear the palm from Idris [Enoch].
Such is his jealousy that if it fell upon the world
 in one moment the two worlds would clash together.
Such is the awe he inspires that if the sun had
 the slightest awareness of it
 it would be lost in an eternal shadow.
Such is the sanctity of his station that from reverence
 none but he may approach near to it.
Such is his empire that necessarily and inevitably
 it can neither decrease nor increase.
Such is his strength that, did he wish so,
 he could in a single instant
 turn the earth and the nine heavens into wax.
Such is the drink that "their Lord will give them to drink"
 that the soul will dip its bread in blood in hope thereof.
So vast is his realm that if the world ceased to exist
 its expanse would not be a single hair's breadth less.
Such is his infinity that the eye of reason and comprehension
 falls to the ground incapable of traversing the distance.

Farid al-Din Attar, *The Book of God*, "Exordium"

> *In his essence God is beyond all our knowing,*
> *all our experiencing;*
> *the attributes which we ascribe to him*
> *are but a pale reflection of his being.*

GOD IS SPIRIT

"GOD is Spirit" [*John*, 4, 24]. Who can listen to the Spirit's titles and
not be lifted up in his soul? He is called the Spirit of God, the Spirit
of Truth who proceeds from the Father, right Spirit, willing Spirit.
His first and most proper title is Holy Spirit, a name most especially appropriate to everything which is incorporeal, purely immaterial
and indivisible... When we hear the word "Spirit" it is impossible for
us to conceive of something whose nature can be circumscribed or
is subject to change or variation, or is like a creature in any way.
Instead, we are compelled to direct our thoughts on high and to think
of an intelligent being, boundless in power, of unlimited greatness,
generous in goodness, whom time cannot measure.

All things thirsting for holiness turn to him; everything living in
virtue never turns away from him. He waters them with his life-giving breath and helps them reach their proper fulfilment. He perfects
all other things and himself lacks nothing; he gives life to all things
and is never depleted. He does not increase by additions, but is
always complete, self-established, and present everywhere. He is the
source of sanctification, spiritual light, who gives illumination to
everyone using his powers to search for the truth – and the illumination he gives is himself. His nature is unapproachable; only
through his goodness are we able to draw near it. He fills all things
with his power, but only those who are worthy may share it. He dis-
tributes his energy in proportion to the faith of the recipient, not confining it to a single share. He is simple in being; his powers are manifold: they are wholly present everywhere and in everything. He is
distributed but does not change. He is shared, yet remains whole.
Consider the analogy of the sunbeam: each person upon whom its
kindly light falls rejoices as if the sun existed for him alone, yet it
illuminates land and sea, and is the master of the atmosphere. In the
same way, the Spirit is given to each one who receives him as if he
were the possession of that person alone, yet he sends forth sufficient grace to fill all the universe. Everything that partakes of his
grace is filled with joy according to its capacity – the capacity of its
nature, not of his power.

The Spirit does not take up his abode in someone's life through a physical approach; how could a corporeal being approach the bodiless one? Instead, the Spirit comes to us when we withdraw ourselves from evil passions, which have crept into the soul through its friendship with the flesh, alienating us from a close relationship with God. Only when a man has been cleansed of the shame of his evil, and has returned to his natural beauty, and the original form of the royal image has been restored in him, is it possible for him to approach the Paraclete. Then, like the sun, he will show you in himself the image of the invisible, and with purified eyes you will see in this blessed image the unspeakable beauty of its prototype.

Through him hearts are lifted up, the infirm are held by the hand and those who progress are brought to spiritual perfection. He shines upon those who are cleansed from every spot and makes them spiritual men through fellowship with himself. When a sunbeam falls on a transparent substance, the substance itself becomes brilliant and radiates light from itself. So too Spirit-bearing souls, illumined by him, finally become spiritual themselves and their grace is sent forth to others. From this comes knowledge of the future, understanding of the mysteries, apprehension of hidden things, distribution of wonderful gifts, heavenly citizenship, a place in the choir of angels, endless joy in the presence of God, becoming like God, and, the highest of all desires, becoming God.

Basil of Caesarea, *On the Holy Spirit*, IX

God is Spirit:
and the Spirit of God is wholly present
in all that is, and reveals himself
to those who are prepared to receive him.

THE SUPREME SELF

I SHALL now declare to thee the true nature of the Supreme Self, knowing which, freed from bondage, a man gains final liberation.

There is a certain eternal Self, on which the consciousness of self-hood rests; this is the witness of the three fields of consciousness; this is other than the five vestures [matter, force, mind, knowledge and bliss].

This is he who perceives all things in waking, dreaming, dream-lessness; this is the true "I" which perceives the intelligence and its activities, whether they be good or evil.

This is he who perceives all, whom none perceives; who illumines the intelligence and the other powers, whom none illumines.

Who penetrates and upholds this universe, whom none penetrates nor upholds; from him this universe derives the light with which it is illumined.

Through whose mere presence the body, powers, mind and intelligence turn to their proper objects as though obeying its command.

By whom, having as his essence eternal wisdom, all the powers from the personality to the body, all objects, all pleasures and pains are seen as a jar is seen.

This inner Self, the Spirit, the ancient, is the presence of primal, undivided joy; ever unchanging, consisting of pure wisdom, by whose command voice and the life-breaths fulfil their parts.

Here, verily, in the Self of Goodness, in the secret place of the soul, in the undivided firmament; rising like the dawn, this shines like the risen sun in the sky, by its radiance making this whole world shine.

Beholding all activities of the mind and personal self, all motions of the body, the powers, the life-breaths, this neither strives nor changes, pervading them like the fire in the heated iron.

This enters not into birth or death or growth, nor does he wane or change for ever; even when this frame falls into dissolution, the Self is not dissolved like the ether in the broken jar.

Standing apart from the vicissitudes of the manifest world, in his own essence pure consciousness, illumining this infinite universe of things enduring and unenduring, himself unchanging, the supreme Self, in the fields of waking, dream and dreamlessness, shines as the true "I", as the immediate witness of the intelligence.

Do thou, with disciplined mind, recognise this Self within thyself, saying, "This is I," through the grace of understanding; cross the shoreless ocean of manifested life whose waves are birth and death, reaching thy goal, coming home to the being of the Eternal.

Shankaracharya, *Vivekachudamani*
(The Crest-Jewel of Discrimination)

The Supreme Self is that which
penetrates, ordains and maintains
all creation, visible and invisible;
that which manifests itself
in the depths of the human soul.

THE COMING ONE

RIGHT down the ages, in many world cycles and in many countries (and today in all) great points of tension have occurred which have been characterised by a hopeful sense of expectancy. Someone is expected and his coming is anticipated. Always in the past, it has been the religious teachers of the period who have fostered and proclaimed this expectancy and the time has always been one of chaos and difficulty, of a climaxing point at the close of a civilisation or culture and when the resources of the old religions have seemed inadequate to meet men's difficulties or to solve their problems. The coming of the avatar, the advent of a Coming One and, in terms of today, the reappearance of the Christ are the keynotes of the prevalent expectancy. When the times are ripe, the invocation of the masses is strident enough and the faith of those who know is keen enough, *then* always he has come and today will be no exception to this ancient rule or to this universal law. For decades, the reappearance of the Christ, the avatar, has been anticipated by the faithful in both hemispheres – not only by the Christian faithful, but by those who look for Maitreya and for the Bodhisattva as well as those who expect the Imam Mahdi.

When men feel that they have exhausted all their own resources and have come to an end of all their own innate possibilities and that the problems and conditions confronting them are beyond their solving or handling, they are apt to look for a divine intermediary and for the mediator who will plead their cause with God and bring about a rescue. They look for a saviour. This doctrine of mediators, of messiahs, of Christs and of avatars can be found running like a golden thread through all the world faiths and scriptures and, relating these world scriptures to some central source of emanation, they are found in rich abundance everywhere. Even the human soul is regarded as an intermediary between man and God; Christ is believed by countless millions to act as the divine mediator between humanity and divinity. [...]

All the world avatars or saviours, however, express two basic incentives: the need for God to contact humanity and to have relationship with men, and the need of humanity for divine contact, help and understanding. Subject to those incentives, all true avatars are therefore divine intermediaries. They can act in this fashion because they have completely divorced themselves from every limitation, from the sense of selfhood and separativeness and are no longer – by ordinary human standards – the dramatic centre of their lives, as are most of us. When they have reached that state of spiritual decentralisation, they themselves can then become *events* in the life of our planet; toward them every eye can look and all men can be affected. Therefore, an avatar or a Christ comes forth for two reasons: one, the inscrutable and unknown cause prompts him so to do, and the other is the demand or the invocation of humanity itself. An avatar is consequently a spiritual event, coming to us to bring about great changes or major restorations, to inaugurate a new civilisation or to restore the "ancient landmarks" and lead man nearer to the divine. They have been defined as "extraordinary men who from time to time appear to change the face of the world and inaugurate a new era in the destinies of humanity." They come in times of crisis; they frequently create crises in order to bring to an end the old and the undesirable and make way for new and more suitable forms for the evolving life of God immanent in nature. They come when evil is rampant. For this reason, if for no other, an avatar may be looked for today. The necessary stage is set for the reappearance of the Christ.

Alice Bailey, *The Reappearance of the Christ*

> *God reaches out to humanity*
> *through divine emissaries: the avatars.*
> *May the Christ be with us*
> *now and forever.*

BRAHMAN IS ALL

WHEN he himself reveals himself
   Brahman brings into manifestation
   that which can never be seen.
As the seed is in the plant,
   as the shade is in the tree,
   as the void is in the sky,
   as infinite forms are in the void -
So from beyond the Infinite, the Infinite comes;
   and from the Infinite the finite extends.
The creature is in Brahman, and Brahman is in the creature:
   they are ever distinct, yet ever united.
He himself is the tree, the seed and the germ.
He himself is the sun, the light, and the lighted.
He himself is Brahman, creature, and Maya.
He himself is manifold form, the infinite space;
He himself is the breath, the word, and the meaning.
He himself is the limit and the limitless:
   and beyond both the limited and the limitless is he,
   the pure Being.
He is the immanent mind in Brahman and in the creature.
The Supreme Soul is seen within the soul,
The Point is seen within the Supreme Soul,
And within the Point, the reflection is seen again.
Kabir is blest because he has this supreme vision!

In the beginning was he alone,
   sufficient unto himself:
   the formless, colourless, and unconditioned Being.
Then was there neither beginning, middle, nor end;
Then were no eyes, no darkness, no light;
Then were no ground, air,
   nor sky, no fire, water, nor earth;
   no rivers like the Ganges and the Junna,
   no seas, oceans and waves.
Then was neither vice nor virtue;
   scriptures there were not,

as the Vedas, and Puranas, nor as the Koran.
Kabir ponders in his mind and says:
   "Then there was no activity:
   the Supreme Being remained merged
   in the unknown depths of his own self."
The Guru neither eats nor drinks, neither lives nor dies;
Neither has he form, line, colour, nor vesture.
He who has neither caste nor clan nor anything else -
   how may I describe his glory?
He has neither form nor formlessness,
He has no name,
He has neither colour nor colourlessness,
He has no dwelling-place.

Kabir, *Poems*

He who is All in All
is before the all;
from the infinity of his pure being
he brings forth the visible
and invisible finite.

BEING

GOD is. That is the primordial fact. It is in order that we may discover this fact for ourselves, by direct experience, that we exist. The final end and purpose of every human being is the unitive knowledge of God's being.

What is the nature of God's being? The invocation to the Lord's Prayer gives us the answer. "Our Father who *art* in heaven." God is, and is ours – immanent in each sentient being, the life of all lives, the spirit animating every soul. But this is not all. God is also the transcendent creator and lawgiver, the Father who loves and, because he loves, also educates his children. And finally, God is "in heaven". That is to say, he possesses a mode of existence which is incommensurable and incompatible with the mode of existence possessed by human beings in their natural, unspiritualized condition. Because he is ours and immanent, God is very close to us. But because he is also in heaven, most of us are very far from God. The saint is one who is as close to God as God is to him.

It is through prayer that men come to the unitive knowledge of God. But the life of prayer is also a life of mortification, of dying to self. It cannot be otherwise; for the more there is of self, the less there is of God. Our pride, our anxiety, our lusts for power and pleasure are God-eclipsing things. So too is that greedy attachment to certain creatures which passes too often for unselfishness and should be called, not altruism, but alter-egoism. And hardly less God-eclipsing is the seemingly self-sacrificing service which we give to any cause or ideal that falls short of the divine. Such service is always idolatry, and makes it impossible for us to worship God as we should, much less to know him. God's kingdom cannot come unless we begin by making our human kingdoms go. Not only the mad and obviously evil kingdoms, but also the respectable ones – the kingdoms of the scribes and pharisees, the good citizens and pillars of society, no less than the kingdoms of the publicans and sinners. God's being cannot be known by us, if we choose to pay our attention and our allegiance to something else, however creditable that something else may seem in the eyes of the world.

Aldous Huxley, "Seven Meditations"

My purpose, and that of
all my fellows,
is to achieve the unitive knowledge of God,
surpassing thereby all things which
keep me from him.

THE ELEMENTAL COSMIC ENERGY

ALL existences are *ku* [void, vacuity]. Existence consists simply of various phenomena within the elemental cosmic energy. It is beyond the physical world and the metaphysical world. Beyond the mater -ial, beyond the spiritual. Only the elemental cosmic energy is absolute. And yet, since we find there no noumenon, this cosmic energy is also ku.

Ku is not empty. Ku conceals terrifying and unlimited powers. The cosmic energy produces, one by one, all the phenomenal exis- tences in the universe; sometimes, too, it destroys them.

In Christianity it is necessary to believe in the notion that God is an absolute personal existence. But I believe that God signifies also the elemental cosmic energy.

We find no substance in God. Nor can we find any personal sub- stantial existence in the universe. Thus God signifies elemental cos- mic energy. This energy can neither diminish nor end. It is with God. God cannot die. Like the elemental cosmic energy, God is the eter- nal absolute.

To believe in the elemental cosmic energy is to have real faith in God. Each one of us is a child of this elemental energy. Each one of us is a cosmic existence. It is this to which we must awaken. "To be awakened", writes Master Dogen in the *Genjo Koan*, "is to be certi- fied by all the existences in the universe."

During zazen, when we abandon our ego, we feel, we experience the union of our bodies with the universe. By means of correct pos- ture, respiration and the consciousness known as *hishiryo* [thinking without thought; beyond thought], we can harmonize ourselves with the universe. Then our ego penetrates the universe and, as this hap- pens, the hishiryo consciousness becomes the entire universe. The plenitude of our consciousness fills the universe. Our ego penetrates God and communicates with him, thus it becomes itself God.

Taisen Deshimaru, *La Voix de la Vallée*

---

*The Eternal Absolute is
elemental cosmic energy, source of all phenomena,
source of each one of us.*

---

2 GOD IS LIGHT

THE POINT OF LIGHT

YOU are the point of light within My mind. You are the point of love within My heart. When you can accept it, when you can see yourself as the microcosm of the macrocosm, you will never again belittle yourself or think ill of yourself. You will realise that you are indeed made in My image and likeness, that we are one, and that nothing and no one can separate us. If you feel any separation from Me, it is of your own making, for I never separate Myself from you. You are individually what I AM universally. Is it any wonder you have to be born again to accept the wonder of this truth? So many souls have strayed so far from Me, and have separated themselves to such an extent that they have placed Me in the heavens at such heights that I AM unapproachable. I AM within you, hidden in the very depths waiting to be recognized and drawn forth.

Eileen Caddy, *Opening Doors Within* (29 May)

> *I am a point of light,*
> *a spark of the divine and eternal light,*
> *which shines forever within me.*

THE LIGHT AND THE ECSTASY

I ENTERED the place where I usually prayed and, mindful of the words of the holy man, I began to say, "Holy God". At once I was so greatly moved to tears and loving desire for God that I would be unable to describe in words the joy and delight I then felt. I fell prostrate to the ground, and at once I saw, and behold, a great Light was immaterially shining on me and seized hold of my whole mind and soul, so that I was struck with amazement at the unexpected marvel and I was, as it were, in ecstasy. Moreover I forgot the place where I stood, who I was, and where, and could only cry out, "Lord, have mercy," so that when I came to myself I discovered that I was reciting this. But father, who it was that was speaking, and who moved my tongue, I do not know – only God knows.

Whether I was in body, or outside the body (*2 Corinthians,* 12), I conversed with this Light. The Light itself knows it; it scattered whatever mist there was in my soul and cast out every earthly care. It expelled from me all material denseness and bodily heaviness that made my members to be sluggish and numb. What an awesome marvel! It so invigorated and strengthened my limbs and muscles, which had been faint through great weariness, that it seemed to me as though I was stripping myself of the garment of corruption. Besides, there was poured into my soul in unutterable fashion a great spiritual joy and perception and a sweetness surpassing every taste of visible objects, together with a freedom and forgetfulness of all thoughts pertaining to this life. In a marvellous way there was granted to me and revealed to me the manner of the departure from this present life. Thus all the perceptions of my mind and my soul were wholly concentrated on the ineffable joy of that Light.

But when that infinite Light which had appeared to me – for I can call it by no other fitting or appropriate name – in some way had gently and gradually faded and, as it were, had withdrawn itself, I regained possession of myself and realized what its power had suddenly done to me. I reflected on its departure and considered how it had left me again to be alone in this life. So severe was the grief and pain that overcame me that I am at a loss properly to describe how great it was: a varied and most vehement pain was kindled like a fire in my heart. Imagine, father, if you can, the pain of being separated from it, the infinity of love, the greatness of my passion, the sublimity of this greatest of blessings! I on my part cannot express in words or comprehend with my mind the infinity of this vision. [...]

Father, when it appears it fills one with joy, when it vanishes it wounds. It happens close to me and carries me up to heaven. It is a pearl [of great price]. The Light envelops me and appears to me like a star, and is incomprehensible to all. It is radiant like the sun, and I perceive all creation encompassed by it. It shows me all that it contains, and enjoins me to respect my own limits. I am hemmed in by roof and walls, yet it opens heavens to me. I lift up my eyes sensibly to contemplate the things that are on high, and I see all things as they were before. I marvel at what has happened, and I hear a voice speaking to me secretly from on high, "These things are but symbols and preliminaries, for you will not see that which is perfect as long as you are clothed in flesh. But return to yourself and see that you do nothing that deprives you of the things that are above. Should you fall, however, it is to recall you to humility! Do not cease to cultivate penitence, for when it is united to my love for mankind it blots out past and present failures."

Symeon the New Theologian, *The Discourses*, XVI

As an immaterial Light is God,
a Light of infinite purity and ineffable joy,
a purifying and comforting Light.

THE LIGHT OF THE HEAVENS AND THE EARTH

GOD is the light of the heavens and the earth. His light may be compared to a niche that enshrines a lamp, the lamp within a crystal of star-like brilliance. It is lit from a blessed olive tree neither eastern nor western. Its very oil would almost shine forth, though no fire touched it. Light upon light; God guides to his light whom he will.

His light is found in temples which God has sanctioned to be built for the remembrance of his name. In them, morning and evening, his praise is sung by men whom neither trade nor profit can divert from remembering him, from offering prayers, or from giving alms; who dread the day when men's hearts and eyes shall write with anguish; who hope that God will requite them for their noblest deeds and lavish his grace upon them. God gives without measure to whom he will.

As for the unbelievers, their works are like a mirage in a desert. The thirsty traveller thinks it is water, but when he comes near he finds that it is nothing. He finds God there, who pays him back in full. Swift is God's reckoning.

Or like darkness on a bottomless ocean spread with clashing billows and overcast with clouds: darkness upon darkness. If he stretches out his hand he can scarcely see it. Indeed the man from whom God withholds his light shall find no light at all. [...]

It is God who has sovereignty over the heavens and the earth. To him shall all things return.

Do you not see how God drives the clouds, then gathers and piles them up in masses which pour down torrents of rain? From heaven's mountains he sends down the hail, pelting with it whom he will and turning it away from whom he pleases. The flash of his lightning almost snatches off men's eyes.

The Koran, Sourate 24 ("Light")

> *God is the light of the world;*
> *he illuminates those whom he will;*
> *without his light, man is but darkness.*

THE LIGHT OF THE SPIRIT

RADIANT in his light, yet invisible in the secret place of the heart, the Spirit is the supreme abode wherein dwells all that moves and breathes and sees. Know him as all that is, and all that is not, the end of love-longing beyond understanding, the highest in all beings.

He is self-luminous and more subtle than the smallest; but in him rest all the worlds and their beings. He is the everlasting Brahman, and he is life and word and mind. He is truth and life immortal. He is the goal to be aimed at: attain that goal, my son!

Take the great bow of the Upanishads and place in it an arrow sharp with devotion. Draw the bow with concentration on him and hit the centre of the mark, the same everlasting Spirit.

The bow is the sacred OM, and the arrow is our own soul. Brahman is the mark of the arrow, the aim of the soul. Even as an arrow becomes one with its mark, let the watchful soul be one in him.

In him are woven the sky and the earth and all the regions of the air, and in him rest the mind and all the powers of life. Know him as the ONE and leave aside all other words. He is the bridge of immortality.

Where all the subtle channels of the body meet, like spokes in the centre of a wheel, there he moves in the heart and transforms his one form unto many. Upon OM, Atman, your Self, place your meditation. Glory unto you in your far-away journey beyond darkness!

He who knows all and sees all, and whose glory the universe shows, dwells as the Spirit of the divine city of Brahman in the region of the human heart. He becomes mind and drives on the body and life, draws power from food and finds peace in the heart. There the wise find him as joy and light and life eternal.

Mundaka Upanishad, II

> *All that is reposes in the Spirit,*
> *the Brahman, the One,*
> *Light of light, the finality*
> *of human striving.*

FIRE AND LIGHT

GOD is the universal life from which all life receives its breath, just
as the sunbeam derives its origin from the sun. And God is the fire
from which that fire directed toward bliss has been enkindled like
sparks emerging from a fire. How fitting – we may ask – would it be
if nothing alive should cling to that life, and if that fire should give
off neither warmth nor light? What would it be like if living creatures did not cling to life, or if life did not give off warmth and illumination? And what if neither life nor brilliance were to emerge
from the Godhead, which was before time was? And how would it
be if the light enkindled by fire were not to give light to men and
women since the fire neither conceals its light nor the sun its rays?
All this is God: the life by which the immense host of angels has
been enkindled like sparks emerging from a fire. And thus it would
be regrettable if this light could not give off any illumination. And
this splendour is eternal since it can know no death.

How are we to understand these things? The Godhead is unique:
it is of itself and within itself. God has not received the divine Being
from an outside source. God is Being itself. And, in fact, all creatures are indebted to God for their existence. [...]

God created us in the light of divine power. God placed us in the
inextinguishable day of Paradise which, without decay, was to live
in fruitfulness. Meanwhile, we humans attempted insubordination
and thus recognized that we were naked. This was a great source of
joy to the devil. The devil had stripped humanity because he himself
had lost the splendour of his beauty. But God appeared in a white
cloud like a flame. At the time God remained alien to the human
species, so to speak, just as God later appeared with a veiled coun-
tenance to Moses and other favoured individuals. God did not want
humanity to remain naked because God intended that the Son would
at some time wear a human garment. [...]

God is the living light in every respect. From God all lights shine.
Therefore, we remain a light that gives off light through God. For we
are fire according to our essence. Therefore, God cooks us in fire
and floods us with water. As a result, and because of the warmth of
human flesh, this water within us is red and flows red. Would it be
according to the plan for us to remain dark – for us who shine from

light? Or would it be right if we could not move – we who live from fire? For if we had creative activity and no stable abode, we should be but an empty thing.

God, who is fire and light, enlivens us through the soul and stirs us through reason. Thus in the sound of the Word God created the whole world, which is our abode. We are thus creatively at work with our essence, just as God formed us perfectly in every respect.

Hildegard of Bingen, *Book of Divine Works*

I am a being of fire,
I am a being of light;
thus has God created me in his image and likeness,
he who is Fire and Light.

HOMAGE TO THE CO-EMERGENT WISDOM

THE DARKNESS that has collected in thousands of kalpas
One torch will dispel.
Likewise, one moment's experience of luminous mind
Will dissolve the veil of karmic impurities. [...]

If you perceive space,
The fixed ideas of centre and boundary dissolve.
Likewise, if mind perceives mind,
All mental activities will cease,
You will remain in a state of non-thought,
And you will realise the supreme bodhicitta.

Vapours arising from the earth become clouds
And then vanish into the sky;
It is not known where the clouds go when they have dissolved.
Likewise, the waves of thoughts derived from mind
Dissolve when mind perceives mind.

Space has neither colour nor shape;
It is changeless, it is not tinged by black or white.
Likewise, luminous mind has neither colour nor shape;
It is not tinged by black or white, virtue or vice.

The sun's pure and brilliant essence
Cannot be dimmed by the darkness
That endures for a thousand kalpas.
Likewise, the luminous essence of mind
Cannot be dimmed by the long kalpas of samsara.

Though it may be said that space is empty,
Space cannot be described.
Likewise, though it may be said that mind is luminous,
Naming it does not prove that it exists.
Space is completely without locality.
Likewise, *mahamudra* [great seal] mind dwells nowhere.

Without change, rest loose in the primordial state;
There is no doubt that your bonds will loosen.
The essence of mind is like space;
Therefore, there is nothing which it does not encompass.

The body, like a hollow bamboo, has no substance.
Mind is like the essence of space, having no place for thoughts.
Rest loose your mind;
Neither hold it nor permit it to wander.
If your mind has no aim, it is *mahamudra*.
Accomplishing this is the attainment of supreme enlightenment.

The nature of the mind is luminous, without object of perception.
You will discover the path of Buddha
 when there is no path of meditation.
By meditating on non-meditation
 you will attain the supreme bodhi. [...]

Having no mind, without desires,
Self-quieted, self-existing,
It is like a wave of water.
Luminosity is veiled only by the rising of desire.

The real vow of *samaya* [tantric commitments] is broken by thinking in terms of precepts.
If you neither dwell, perceive, nor stray from the ultimate,
Then you are the holy practitioner,
The torch which illuminates darkness.

Tilopa, "Mahamudra Upadesa"

---

*The real nature of my spirit is luminous;
though this luminosity becomes obscured
in this world of illusion,
its essence remains ever the same.*

GOD DWELLS IN THE LIGHT

THE SCRIPTURE says, "God is light, and in him is no darkness at all."
Therefore the scripture affirms light to be superior, and absolutely
separate from, and eternally antecedent to darkness. In this scripture
you have a noble and true account of light, what it is, where it is, and
was, and always must be. It can never change its state or place, be
altered in itself, be anywhere, or in another manner, than as it was,
and will be, from eternity to eternity. When God said, "Let there be
light," and "there was light", no change happened to eternal light
itself, nor did any light then begin to be; but the darkness of this
world then only began to receive a power, or operation of the eternal light upon it, which it had not before; or eternity then began to
open some resemblance of its own glory in the dark elements, and
shadows of time, and thus it is, that I assert the priority and glory of
light, and put all darkness under its feet, as impossible to be any
thing else but its footstool. [...]

The scripture says that "God dwells in the light, to which no man
can approach": therefore the scripture teaches, that light in itself is,
and must be invisible to man; that it cannot be approached, or made
manifest to him, but in and by something that is not light. And this
is all that I said, when I affirmed, that light cannot be manifested, or
have any visibility to created eyes, but in and through and by the
darkness.

Light, as it is in itself, is only in the supernatural Deity; and that
is the reason, why no man, or any created being, can approach to it,
or have any sensibility of it, as it is in itself. And yet no light can
come into this world, but that in which God dwelt before any world
was created. No light can be in time, but that which was the light of
eternity. If therefore the supernatural light is to manifest something
of its incomprehensible glory, and make itself in some degree sensible and visible to the creature, this supernatural light must enter into
nature, it must put on materiality. Now darkness is the one only
materiality of light, in and through which it can become the object
of creaturely eyes; and till then there is darkness, there is no possible medium or power through which the supernatural light can manifest something of itself, or have any of its glory visible to created
eyes. And the reason why darkness can only be the materiality of all

nature, and of all materiality, whether in heaven or on earth. And therefore every thing that is creatively in nature, that has any form, figure or substance, from the highest angel in heaven to the lowest thing upon earth, has all that it has of figure, form or substantiality, only and solely from darkness.

William Law, *The Spirit of Love*

Visible in the darkness of the material universe, the light which we see is a reflection of the pure and supernatural eternal light of God.

YOU HAVE SEEN THE LIGHTNING

YOU have seen the lightning...
    keep your secret.
Lightning ripped asunder the clouds
    and revealed the depths to you.
Lightning ripped asunder the heavens
    which you discovered in your soul.
Lightning ripped asunder the firmament
    you have no shelter.
Lightning ripped asunder your own self
    it never returned.
But you know that you are beyond the darkness
    keep your secret.
For those who have not seen the lightning will think
    that you speak of the fire here below.

You have seen the lightning...
    keep your secret.
People will ask why
    and will not understand
    and will condemn you.
They will not understand that the sky
    was ripped asunder for you
    and that you are no longer
    on this side of the firmament.
Live happy and smiling in this world
    infinitely free.

The sky was torn open for Jesus at his baptism
    and he heard the inner voice.
When the sky is torn open
    the only prayer is the prayer of truth.
As long as the sky of your heart is not torn open
    by the lightning-bolt of Sinai,
    the storm of Pentecost,
    you know nothing of God,
    you call God this firmament, limit of your thought. [...]

Keep your secret.
You can say nothing more
    therefore say nothing.
Do not descend further
    remain in your "self".
But who speaks this?
And to whom does he speak?

Henri Le Saux, "Diary", 9 May 1970

> *The lightning-bolt of God*
> *tears apart my soul:*
> *everything changes in this instant;*
> *I am no longer myself.*

LIGHT AND ILLUMINATION

REAL light does not glitter; it does not shine in a spectacular fashion like fame. [...] For Western people, the word "illumination" suggests something extraordinarily brilliant. But true light does not shine on the exterior; it is not blinding.

Shinku, in Japanese, means true illumination which does not dazzle. It is a koan. Not to show one's light on the outside. To discover the original light in the foundations of one's heart. Unconsciously, to discover, through meditation in zazen, the intuition of original existence. To receive energy into one's body and spirit – into each and every cell. Of course, the Buddha achieved illumination and this illumination is symbolically represented by a mark on his forehead, between the eyes, the third eye. Everyone knows this. But in zen illumination also means "not to eat with the nose, but with the mouth", that is to say, not to make false gestures. Illumination shines through every gesture of daily life.

Illumination is thus not only brilliant, but it can also be sombre. Sometimes long and sometimes short, sometimes square and sometimes round! The clear light shines forth in the dark of night and the marvellous lotus flowers in the mud of the marshes. A great master achieved enlightenment upon hearing a pebble resound on a bamboo, and another on seeing a peach tree in flower. Newton realized a scientific insight seeing an apple fall from an apple-tree, and Archimedes in his bath. Illumination, the "great intuition", also flows "from my soul to your soul" (*i shin den shin*), in the contact with another, in the communication from spirit to spirit. Light is everywhere. "A cloud rises on the South Mountain, it rains on the North Mountain", says a famous koan.

The great wisdom consists in achieving harmony with the universe. Illumination arises when the conscious ego becomes cosmic truth. In zen, we speak of enlightenment or *satori*. There is nothing, however, to be sought. By practising zazen regularly *satori* can be achieved automatically, sometimes gradually, sometimes in a complete internal revolution, a total reorientation of the self towards the interior. Pure light without blemish is the highest wisdom, without suffering, without ignorance, without doubts, without worry. Each phenomenon of our lives, every day, opens the door. The fire still burns in the middle of the glowing embers. If we penetrate unceasingly into the soil of our spirit, surely we will find the bubbling spring, the profound wisdom which encompasses all things.

The brilliant moonlight of the spirit, pure,
without blemish, without fault, shatters
on the waves lapping the shore
and floods it with light.

True cosmic light, beyond time and space, eternal light. A star twinkles in the evening sky, a minute point in the great, tranquil, silent ocean of emptiness. Light has shone in the dark void and the round has commenced. Energy, matter, life, conscience, void... Thus does being return to its origin, motion ceases, everything is calm. Every one of us is a particle endowed with consciousness, a delicate, fragile light, a flash of existence destined for death, surging forth from the absolute void like the star shining in the night sky. If we ignore the illusory nature of the Self, we do not truly know ourselves. Enlightenment comes from this knowledge. The little cinder in the midst of the ashes is like the solitary star, or the real Self which manifests itself in meditation. The holy night is light, and the real God is within this holy night, which shines more brilliantly than the sun.

Taisen Deshimaru, *La Pratique du Zen*

True illumination is understanding
of ultimate reality;
it shines in the depths of the spirit,
and manifests itself in every gesture.

THE LIGHT OF THE WORLD

"I AM the light of the world." Who is the light of the world except God's Son? This, then, is merely a statement of the truth about yourself. It is the opposite of a statement of pride, of arrogance, or of self-deception. It does not describe the self concept you have made. It does not refer to any of the characteristics with which you have endowed your idols. It refers to you as you were created by God. It simply states the truth.

To the ego, today's idea is the epitome of self-glorification. But the ego does not understand humility, mistaking it for self-debasement. Humility consists of accepting your role in salvation and in taking no other. It is not humility to insist you cannot be the light of the world if that is the function God assigned to you. It is only arrogance that would assert this function cannot be for you, and arrogance is always of the ego.

True humility requires that you accept today's idea because it is God's voice which tells you it is true. This is the beginning step in accepting your real function on earth. It is a giant stride toward taking your rightful place in salvation. It is a positive assertion of your right to be saved, and an acknowledgement of the power that is given you to save others.

You will want to think about this idea as often as possible today. It is the perfect answer to all illusions, and therefore to all temptation. It brings all the images you have made about yourself to the truth, and helps you depart in peace, unburdened and certain of your purpose.

As many practice periods as possible should be undertaken today, although each one need not exceed a minute or two. They should begin with telling yourself:

> *I am the light of the world.*
> *That is my only function.*
> *That is why I am here.* [...]

"Forgiveness is my function as the light of the world." It is your forgiveness that will bring the world of darkness to the light. It is your forgiveness that lets you recognize the light in which you see.

Forgiveness is the demonstration that you are the light of the world. Through your forgiveness does the truth about yourself return to your memory. Therefore, in your forgiveness lies your salvation.

Illusions about yourself and the world are one. That is why all forgiveness is a gift to yourself. Your goal is to find out who you are, having denied your identity by attacking creation and its Creator. Now you are learning how to remember the truth. For this attack must be replaced by forgiveness, so that thoughts of life may replace thoughts of death.

Remember that in every attack you call upon your own weakness, while each time you forgive you call upon the strength of Christ in you. Do you not then begin to understand what forgiveness will do for you? It will remove all sense of weakness, strain and fatigue from your mind. It will take away all fear and guilt and pain. It will restore the invulnerability and power God gave his Son to your awareness.

Let us be glad to begin and end this day by practising today's idea, and to use it as frequently as possible throughout the day. It will help to make the day as happy for you as God wants you to be. And it will help those around you, as well as those who seem to be far away in space and time, to share this happiness with you.

As often as you can, closing your eyes if possible, say to yourself today:

> *Forgiveness is my function as the light of the world.*
> *I would fulfil my function that I may be happy.*

A Course in Miracles

> *I am a child of God,*
> *bearing within me the light of divinity:*
> *this light shines in the world*
> *and manifests itself as forgiveness.*

THE LIGHT OF THE PURE MIND

THIS pure Mind, the source of everything, shines forever and on all with the brilliance of its own perfection. But the people of the world do not awake to it, regarding only that which sees, hears, feels and knows as mind. Blinded by their own sight, hearing, feeling and knowing, they do not perceive the spiritual brilliance of the source-substance. If they would only eliminate all conceptual thought in a flash, that source-substance would manifest itself like the sun ascending through the void and illuminating the whole universe without hindrance or bounds.

Therefore, if you students of the Way seek to progress through seeing, hearing, feeling and knowing, when you are deprived of your perceptions, your way to Mind will be cut off and you will find nowhere to enter. Only realize that, though real Mind is expressed in these perceptions, it neither forms part of them nor is separate from them. You should not start REASONING from these perceptions, nor allow them to give rise to conceptual thought; yet nor should you seek the One Mind apart from them or abandon them in your pursuit of the dharma. Do not keep them nor abandon them nor dwell in them nor cleave to them. Above, below and around you, all is spontaneously existing, for there is nowhere which is outside the Buddha-Mind.

Huang Po, *On the Transmission of Mind*, 9

The pure Mind, beyond yet within
all seeing, hearing, feeling and knowing,
shines of its own brilliance
throughout the entire universe.

THE DEWDROP

THE IMAGE of the morning sun in a dewdrop is not less than the sun. The reflection of life in your soul is not less than life.

The dewdrop mirrors the light because it is one with light, and you reflect life because you and life are one.

When darkness is upon you, say: "This darkness is dawn not yet born; and though night's travail be full upon me, yet shall dawn be born unto me even as unto the hills."

The dewdrop rounding its sphere in the dusk of the lily is not unlike yourself, gathering your soul in the heart of God.

Shall a dewdrop say: "But once in a thousand years am I even a dewdrop," speak you and answer it saying: "Know you not that the light of all the years is shining in your circle?"

Kahlil Gibran, *The Garden of the Prophet*

The dewdrop shines with the same brilliance
as the sun itself;
the life in my soul shines with the same light
as eternal life.

THE SPLENDOUR OF THE ETERNAL

ARISE, shine; for your light has come,
and the glory of the Lord has risen upon you.

For darkness shall cover the earth,
and thick darkness the peoples;
but the Lord will rise upon you,
and his glory will appear over you.

Nations shall come to your light,
and kings to the brightness of your dawn.
Lift up your eyes and look around;
they all gather together, they come to you;
your sons shall come from far away,
and your daughters shall be carried on their nurses' arms.

Then you shall see and be radiant;
your heart shall thrill and rejoice,
because the abundance of the sea shall be brought to you,
the wealth of the nations shall come to you. [...]

I will appoint Peace as your overseer
and Righteousness as your taskmaster,
Violence shall no more be heard in your land,
devastation or destruction within your borders;
you shall call your walls Salvation
and your gates Praise.

The sun shall no longer be your light by day,
nor for brightness shall the moon give light to you by night;
but the Lord will be your everlasting light,
and your God will be your glory.

Your sun shall no more go down,
or your moon withdraw itself;
for the Lord will be your everlasting light,
and your days of mourning shall be ended.

Your people shall all be righteous;
they shall possess the land forever.
They are the shoot that I planted, the work of my hands,
so that I might be glorified.
The least of them shall become a clan,
and the smallest one a mighty nation.

I am the Lord;
in its time I will accomplish it quickly.

Isaiah, 60

> *May the splendour of the Lord*
> *shine upon you forever,*
> *you and all his people;*
> *the eternal light and peace of the Lord.*

THE VISION OF GLORY

THE SUPREME, the Lord of all mystic power, the Personality of Godhead, displayed his universal form to Arjuna.

Arjuna saw in that universal form unlimited mouths and unlimited eyes. It was all wondrous. The form was decorated with divine, dazzling ornaments and arrayed in many garbs. He was garlanded gloriously... All was magnificent, all-expanding, unlimited. This was seen by Arjuna. If hundreds of thousands of suns rose at once into the sky, they might resemble the effulgence of the Supreme Person in that universal form. At that time Arjuna could see in the universal form of the Lord the unlimited expansions of the universe situated in one place although divided into many, many thousands. [...]

Arjuna began to pray with folded hands, offering obeisance to the Supreme Personality of Godhead. Arjuna said: My dear Lord, Krishna, I see in your body all the demigods and different kinds of living entities, assembled together. I see Brahma sitting on the lotus flower, as well as Lord Shiva and many sages and divine snakes. O Lord of the universe, I see in your universal body many, many forms – arms, bellies, mouths, eyes – expanded without limit. There is no end, there is no beginning, and there is no middle to all this. Your form is very hard to see on account of its glowing effulgence, which is fiery and immeasurable like the sun.

You are the supreme primal objective; you are the best in all the universes; you are inexhaustible, and you are the oldest. You are the maintainer of religion, the eternal Personality of Godhead. You are the origin, without beginning, middle or end. You have numberless arms, and the sun and moon are among your great, unlimited eyes. By your own radiance you are heating this entire universe. Although you are one, you are spread throughout the sky and the planets and in all space between.

Bhagavad Gita, 11

> *Our eyes cannot see,*
> *nor our minds comprehend,*
> *the beauty and brilliance*
> *of the Lord in glory.*

THE POINT OF LIGHT

FROM the point of light within the mind of God
Let light stream forth into the minds of men.
Let light descend on earth.

From the point of love within the heart of God
Let love stream forth into the hearts of men.
May Christ return to earth.

From the centre where the will of God is known
Let purpose guide the little wills of men -
The purpose which the Masters know and serve.

From the centre which we call the race of men
Let the plan of love and light work out.
And may it seal the door where evil dwells.

Let light and love and power
  restore the plan on earth.

Alice Bailey, "The Great Invocation"

*May the light and love
and will of God
be realised on earth.*

3 GOD IS LOVE

THE COMPASSIONATE AND THE MERCIFUL

IN the name of God,
  the Compassionate,
  the Merciful.
Praise be to God,
  Lord of the Universe,
  the Compassionate,
  the Merciful,
Sovereign of the Day of Judgement!
You alone we worship,
  and to you alone
  we turn for help.
Guide us to the straight path,
The path of those whom you have favoured,
Not of those who have incurred your wrath,
Nor of those who have gone astray.

The Koran, "The Exordium"

O God of mercy and compassion,
lead us unto
your mercy and compassion.

THE CANTICLE OF LOVE

THE BELOVED

Let him kiss me with the kisses of his mouth!
For your love is better than wine,
  your anointing oils are fragrant,
Your name is perfume poured out;
  therefore the maidens love you.
Draw me after you, let us make haste.
The king has brought me into his chambers.
We will exult and rejoice in you;
  we will extol your love more than wine;
  rightly do they love you.

The voice of my beloved! Look, he comes,
  leaping upon the mountains, bounding over the hills.
My beloved is like a gazelle or a young stag.
Look, there he stands behind our wall,
Gazing in at the windows, looking through the lattice.
My beloved speaks and says to me:
"Arise, my love, my fair one, and come away;
For now winter is past, the rain is over and gone.
The flowers appear on the earth;
  the time of singing has come,
And the voice of the turtledove is heard in our land.
The fig tree puts forth its figs, and the vines are in blossom;
They give forth fragrance.
Arise, my love, my fair one, and come away.
O my dove, in the clefts of the rock, in the covert of the cliff,
Let me see your face, let me hear your voice;
For your voice is sweet and your face is lovely."

My beloved is mine and I am his;
  he pastures his flock among the lilies.
Until the day breathes and the shadows flee,
Turn, my beloved, be like a gazelle
  or a young stag on the cleft mountains.

THE LOVER

How beautiful you are, my love, how very beautiful!
Your eyes are doves behind your veil.
Your hair is like a flock of goats,
     moving down the slopes of Gilead.
Your teeth are like a flock of shorn ewes
     that have come up from the washing,
All of which bear twins, and not one of them is bereaved.
Your lips are like a crimson thread,
     and your mouth is lovely.
Your cheeks are like halves of a pomegranate behind your veil.
Your neck is like to the tower of David, built in courses;
     on it hang a thousand bucklers, all of them shields of warriors.
Your breasts are like two fawns, twins of a gazelle,
     that feed among the lilies.
Until the day breathes and the shadows flee,
I will hasten to the mountain of myrrh
     and the hill of frankincense.
You are altogether beautiful, my love;
     there is no flaw in you.

You have ravished my heart, my sister, my bride,
You have ravished my heart with a glance of your eyes,
     with one jewel of your necklace.
How sweet is your love, my sister, my bride!
How much better is your love than wine,
     and the fragrance of your oils than any spice!
Your lips distil nectar, my bride;
     honey and milk are under your tongue;
The scent of your garments is like the scent of Lebanon.

THE BELOVED

Upon my bed at night I sought him whom my soul loves;
 I sought him, but found him not.
I called him, but he gave no answer.
"I will rise now and go about the city,

in the streets and in the squares;
I will seek him whom my soul loves."
I sought him, but found him not.
The sentinels found me, as they went about in the city.
"Have you seen him whom my soul loves?"
Scarcely had I passed them,
    when I found him whom my soul loves.
I held him, and would not let him go
    until I brought him into my mother's house,
    and into the chamber of her that conceived me.

I am my beloved's, and his desire is for me.
Come, my beloved, let us go forth into the fields,
    and lodge in the villages;
Let us go out early to the vineyards,
    and see whether the vines have budded,
Whether the grape blossoms have opened
    and the pomegranates are in bloom.
There I will give you my love.

Set me as a seal upon your heart,
    as a seal upon your arm;
For love is strong as death,
    passion fierce as the grave.
Its flashes are flashes of fire,
    a raging flame.
Many waters cannot quench love,
    neither can floods drown it.
If one offered for love all the wealth of his house,
    it would be utterly scorned.

The Song of Songs, passim

> *The Beloved seeks her Beloved,*
> *as he seeks his Beloved;*
> *so the human soul seeks God,*
> *as God seeks the human soul;*
> *what joy is theirs when they are united!*

I HAVE CALLED YOU

BELOVED,
Many times have I called you,
   and you have not heard me.
Many times have I revealed myself to you
   and you have not see me.
Many times have I exuded sweet fragrances,
   and you have not enjoyed me,
Offered you flavoursome food,
   and you have not savoured me.

Why can you not perceive me through the objects you sense?
Or breathe me in the odours?
Why do you not see me?
Why do you not hear me?
Why? Why? Why?

For you my delights surpass all other delights,
   and the pleasures which I give you exceed all others.
For you I am preferable to all possessions.
I am Beauty. I am Grace.

Beloved, Beloved, love me alone, love me with your love.
None is more intimate than I.
Others love you for themselves;
I love you for yourself alone, and you flee far from me.

Beloved, you cannot be my equal,
   because if you draw near to me,
   it is because I have drawn near to you.
I am closer to you than you are to yourself,
   than your soul, than your breath.

Ibn Al-Arabi

> *Beloved: I call out to you,*
> *I reach out for you, in a hundred different ways:*
> *Why do you not answer me? Why?*

LOVE WILL NOT PASS

IF I speak in the tongues of mortals and of angels, but do not have love, I am a noisy gong or a clanging cymbal. And if I have prophetic powers, and understand all mysteries and all knowledge, and if I have all faith, so as to move mountains, but do not have love, I am nothing. If I give away all my possessions, and if I hand over my body so that I may boast, but do not have love, I gain nothing.

Love is patient; love is kind; love is not envious or boastful or arrogant or rude. It does not insist on its own way; it is not irritable or resentful; it does not rejoice in wrongdoing, but rejoices in the truth. It bears all things, believes all things, hopes all things, endures all things.

Love never ends. But as for prophecies, they will come to an end; as for tongues, they will cease; as for knowledge, it will come to an end. For we know only in part, and we prophesy only in part; but when the complete comes, the partial will come to an end. When I was a child, I spoke like a child, I thought like a child, I reasoned like a child; when I became an adult, I put an end to childish ways. For now we see in a mirror, dimly, but then we will see face to face. Now I know only in part; then I will know fully, even as I have been fully known.

And now faith, hope, and love abide, these three; and the greatest of these is love.

First Epistle to the Corinthians, 13

> *Love is the way which surpasses all others;*
> *love will remain when all things*
> *of this world pass away.*

FOLLOW LOVE

WHEN love beckons to you, follow him, though his ways are hard and steep. And when his wings enfold you, yield to him, though the sword hidden among his pinions may wound you. And when he speaks to you, believe in him, though his voice may shatter your dreams as the north wind lays waste the garden.

For even as love crowns you so shall he crucify you. Even as he is for your growth so is he for your pruning. Even as he ascends to your height and caresses your tenderest branches that quiver in the sun, so shall he descend to your roots and shake them in their clinging to the earth.

Like sheaves of corn he gathers you unto himself. He threshes you to make you naked. He sifts you to free you from your husks. He grinds you to whiteness. He kneads you until you are pliant; and then he assigns you to his sacred fire, that you may become sacred bread for God's sacred feast.

All these things shall love do unto you that you may know the secrets of your heart, and in that knowledge become a fragment of Life's heart.

But if in your fear you would seek only love's peace and love's pleasure, then it is better for you that you cover your nakedness and pass out of love's threshing-floor, into the seasonless world where you shall laugh, but not all of your laughter, and weep, but not all of your tears.

Love gives naught but itself and takes naught but from itself.

Love possesses not nor would it be possessed; for love is sufficient unto love.

When you love you should not say, "God is in my heart," but rather, "I am in the heart of God."

And think not you can direct the course of love, for love, if it finds you worthy, directs your course.

Love has no other desire but to fulfil itself. But if you love and must needs have desires, let these be your desires:

To melt and be like a running brook that sings its melody to the night.

To know the pain of too much tenderness.

To be wounded by your own understanding of love, and to bleed willingly and joyfully.

To wake at dawn with a winged heart and give thanks for another day of loving.

To rest at the noon hour and meditate love's ecstasy.

To return home at eventide with gratitude.

And then to sleep with a prayer for the beloved in your heart and a song of praise upon your lips.

Kahlil Gibran, The Prophet, "Love"

> *Rejoice in the happiness of love;*
> *rejoice in the pain of love:*
> *thus will you follow love*
> *and love will fulfil itself in you.*

THE PATH OF LOVE

BHAKTI-YOGA is a real, genuine search after the Lord, a search
beginning, continuing, and ending in love. One single moment of
the madness of extreme love of God brings us eternal freedom.
"Bhakti", says Narada in the *Bhakti Sutras*, "is intense love of God";
"When a man attains it, he loves all, hates none; he becomes satisfied forever"; "This love cannot be reduced to any earthly benefit",
because so long as worldly desires last, that kind of love does not
subsist.

"Bhakti is greater than karma, greater than yoga, because these
are intended for an object in view, while bhakti is its own fruition,
its own means and its own end." [...] There is not really so much difference between knowledge (*jnana-yoga*) and love (*bhakti-yoga*) as
people sometimes imagine... In the end they converge and meet at
the same point. So also it is with *raja-yoga*, which when pursued as
a means to attain liberation..., leads us also to the same goal. [...]

The best definition of bhakti-yoga is perhaps embodied in the
verse: "May that love undying which the non-discriminating have
for the fleeting objects of the senses never leave this heart of mine –
of me who seek after Thee!" (*Vishnu Purana*). We see what a strong
love men who do not know any better have for sense-objects, for
money, dress, their wives, children, friends and possessions. What a
tremendous clinging they have to all these things! So in the above
prayer the sage says, "I will have that attachment, that tremendous
clinging, only to Thee." This love, when given to God, is called
bhakti. Bhakti is not destructive; it teaches us that no one of the
facilities we have has been given in vain, that through them is the
natural way to come to liberation. Bhakti does not kill our tendencies, it does not go against nature, but only gives it a higher and
more powerful direction. How naturally we love the objects of the
senses! We cannot but do so, because they are so real to us. We do
not ordinarily see anything real about higher things, but when a man
has seen something real beyond the senses, beyond the universe of
senses, the idea is that he can have a strong attachment, only it
should be transferred to the object beyond the senses, which is God.
And when the same kind of love that has before been given to sense-
objects is given to God, it is called bhakti. [...]

Bhakti-yoga teaches how to love, without any ulterior motives, loving God and loving the good because it is good to do so, not for going to heaven, nor to get children, wealth, or anything else. It teaches them that love itself is the highest recompense of love – that God himself is love. It teaches them to pay all kinds of tribute to God as the Creator, the Omnipresent, the Omniscient, the Almighty Ruler, the Father and the Mother. The highest praise that can express him, the highest idea that the human mind can conceive of him, is that he is the God of love. Wherever there is love, it is he. "Wherever there is any love, it is he, the Lord who is present there." Where the husband kisses the wife, he is there in the kiss; where the mother kisses the child, he is there in the kiss; where friends clasp hands, he, the Lord, is present as the God of love. When a great man loves and wishes to help mankind, the Lord is there giving freely his bounty out of his love to mankind. Wherever the heart expands, he is there manifested. This is what the bhakti-yoga teaches.

Swami Vivekananda, *Bhakti-Yoga*

> *The most sublime path is that of love:*
> *from attachment to sensual objects*
> *may I realise never-ending love of God*
> *as the God of Love.*

THE HIDDEN TREASURE

FROM *love are we issued;*
According to love are we made;
Towards love we tend;
To love we devote ourselves.

By his divine love, God loves us for ourselves and for himself.
The love by which he loves us for his own sake is based on this holy
hadith: "I was a (hidden) treasure and I was not known. But I desired
to be known. Therefore I created the world in order that I might
make myself known to my creatures. Thus they have known me." It
can be seen from this that God created us for himself so that we
might know him. The following verse is relevant in this respect: "I
created mankind and the *jinn* [spirit-beings] that they might worship
me" (*Koran*, 51). Consequently, he created us for himself alone.

The love which God has for us is expressed through the teachings
which he gives us so that we may act in a fitting manner to come to
beatitude, and which preserve us from actions which do not befit our
nature and purpose.

God – glory to him – made creatures in order that they might
glorify him. He destined them to glorify and praise him and prostrate
themselves before him. This is how we come to know him. Thus he
speaks: "The seven heavens, the earth, and all who dwell in them
give glory to him. All creatures celebrate his praises" (*Koran*, 17).
Praise is thus due to God for his essential nature and his creation.
This mode of knowledge is confirmed by another verse: "Do you not
see how God is praised by those in heaven and those on earth? The
very birds praise him as they wing their flight. He notes the prayers
and praises of all his creatures, and has knowledge of all their
actions" (*Koran*, 24) [...]

God has made known his love for us for our well-being both in
this life and in that to come. He has lavished upon us the proofs of
his science so that we may know him and not that we may ignore
him. He also provides for our needs and bestows his favours on us,
though we are inattentive, despite our awareness of these, and our
knowledge that every kind of goodness by which we act arises solely from his act of creation and should be attributed to him. We

should add that God has granted us these favours in order that we may benefit from them and that we may act in consequence, without being unduly preoccupied to ensure the tranquillity of the soul.

And yet, despite all these gifts from which we benefit, we are ungrateful to him, although reason alone should oblige us to give thanks to him who has provided them for us and despite our knowing that God alone is our benefactor. [...]

The love which God has for his servants has neither beginning nor end... In consequence, the love which he bears for his servants, from the first to the last, by a process without end, is in its essence the very principle of their existence. This is the reason that the love which God has for them is intimately related to his being, which remains inseparable from them, whatever their virtual or actual condition; for God is with them in their actual condition as he is with them in their virtual condition, since they are known to him who contemplates and loves them unceasingly. No new attribute that God does not already possess can be accorded to him. Furthermore, God has never ceased loving his creatures in such a way that, in the divine words of the Prophet, "...I desired to be known...", God has made known to us how the loving act of creation occurs such as it pleases his divine Majesty, since God can only be apprehended by the intellect as agent and creator.

Ibn Al-Arabi, *The Meccan Illuminations*

> *God created us for himself, out of love;*
> *he loves us without limit and without end,*
> *so that in turn we may love him.*

THE SUTRAS OF DIVINE LOVE

THE PATH of bhakti is the path of devotion to God, of divine love. Bhakti is intense love of God; it is the nectar of eternity. Those who achieve this supreme love are perfected, immortal, fulfilled; they are beyond desire, grief, hatred, gaiety, beyond self-seeking. Intoxicated with divine love, they attain overwhelming joy, peace and self-realization.

Bhakti is not motivated by selfish desire, but is renunciation of desire, renunciation by which the lover of God consecrates all worldly and religious activities to him, seeks unity with God and abandons all that leads away from him, all other refuges. Abandon therefore everything that is antagonistic to the Lord: but perform secular and sacred actions of devotion. Observe the prescriptions of scripture while deepening the spiritual life; otherwise, you may lose what you have gained. Attend to those social customs and usages and meet physical needs essential to maintain life.

Divine love is described in different ways: according to the disciple of Parasara, bhakti consists in ardour in worship; according to the sage Garga, it is praising divine glory and greatness; and according to the sage Sandilya, bhakti is found in the enjoyment of bliss of one's true self. But the sage Narada believes that bhakti is the total consecration of all one's activities to God, and extreme anguish if he is at all absent from one's consciousness. [...]

The path of divine love is above those of action (*karma*), knowledge (*jnana*), and (*raja*) yoga: for it is the fruit of these, an end in itself. So, too, does the Lord dislike pride and love humility. For some believe that knowledge alone is sufficient to achieve divine love, while others believe that both are required. According to Narada, bhakti is its own fruit. As knowledge of the king's household, feeding and other favours, is not the same as becoming king or realizing the king's favour or satisfying hunger, so the seekers of liberation should follow only the path which results in divine love.

The sages of the past have taught the ways of fostering bhakti. Love of God is realized through renunciation of the objects of the senses, detachment from the world, ceaseless adoration of the Lord, hearing and reciting the glories of the Lord, even in everyday life: but the surest paths are the grace of the Holy Ones who have attained divine love, and the slightest touch of divine grace itself. And though contact with such Holy Ones is difficult to attain, once it is achieved, their subtle touch is unerringly effective. The grace of God permits communion with such Great Teachers; between God and his true devotee, there is no distinction. Therefore cultivate love of God, love of God alone. [...]

Who is he who crosses the ocean of illusion? He who has renounced attachment to desire, who serves the Holy Ones, who has renounced material possessions; he who seeks retirement from the world, roots out worldly bonds, transcends the three modes of nature (*gunas*), abandons all ideas of acquisition and possession; he who renounces the fruit of action, who dedicates all his activities to God, and thereby becomes free from both suffering and joy; he who renounces even the injunctions of the Vedas to devote himself to the undivided and uninterrupted love of God: he it is who crosses the ocean of illusion, leading others with him.

Words cannot describe the essential nature of divine love; it is like the pleasure of sweetness to a dumb man, this love which manifests itself in those who have become fit receptacles. Beyond telling, this love is above desire; growing ceaselessly, it is more subtle than the subtlest, and is known only by being experienced. Imbued with this love, the devotee sees nothing else, hears nothing else, speaks nothing else, thinks nothing else, save love of God. [...]

The path of divine love is easier than any other. For the proof of love is love itself; love of God brings peace and supreme joy. The devotee has no cause for anxiety over worldly things, since he has surrendered his own self and his temporal and spiritual interests to the Lord. Achievement of bhakti does not mean neglect of life in the world, but renunciation of the fruits of worldly activity. The aspirant should not listen to idle talk about lust, wealth and the activities of unbelievers; conceit and arrogance also have no place for the bhakta. The devotee who has dedicated all to God shares his desires, anger or pride with him alone.

Pass beyond the lower forms of devotion, and cultivate and practise love of God alone, as the love of a devoted servant or wife. True devotees of God love God alone for his own sake; they converse about God with a choking voice, tears in their eyes and a trembling body. They purify their families and the entire earth; they impart sanctity to holy places, render actions righteous, and give authority to scripture, for they are filled with the presence of God. The ancestors rejoice, the gods dance in joy and the earth is blessed with salvation. In them, there are no distinctions of caste, sex, learning, appearance, family or wealth, because they are of God. [...]

God will surely reveal himself to those who love him, filling his devotees with his presence. Love of God alone is the greatest truth: then, now and forever.

Love of God is one, but its forms are many: glorification of God's qualities and attributes; exaltation of his beauty; adoration; constant remembrance of him; loving service to him; love as that of a friend, a child, a wife; surrender to the divine will; complete absorption in him; embracing the anguish of separation from him. [...]

He who believes in this auspicious teaching of Narada and practises it, he will surely become imbued with the love of God; he will realize the beloved Lord and attain the highest beatitude.

Narada, *Bhakti Sutras*

Love of God is the supreme path:
seek therefore detachment from the world and purification,
that you may abide in the love of God
and be filled with his divine presence.

THE LIVING FLAME OF LOVE

O LIVING flame of love
That tenderly wounds my soul
In its deepest centre! Since
Now you are not oppressive,
Now consummate! if it be your will:
Tear through the veil of this sweet encounter!

O sweet cautery,
O delightful wound!
O gentle hand! O delicate touch
That tastes of eternal life
And pays every debt!
In killing you changed death to life.

O lamps of fire!
In whose splendours
The deep caverns of feeling,
Once obscure and blind,
Now give forth, so rarely, so exquisitely,
Both warmth and light to their Beloved.

How gently and lovingly
You wake in my heart,
Where in secret you dwell alone;
And in your sweet breathing,
Filled with good and glory,
How tenderly you swell my heart with love.

John of the Cross,
"Stanzas the soul recites in intimate union with God"

> *The living flame of your love*
> *burns me with its heat,*
> *and illuminates your presence*
> *in my heart, O my God.*

THE LORD OF COMPASSION

IN the Buddhas, dharma and supreme assembly I seek refuge until enlightenment. May I, through merit gained by gifts and other virtues, accomplish Buddhahood for the sake of all beings.

On the crown of my head and all sentient beings pervading space, there rests the letter HRI on a white lotus and a moon seat. From this letter appears the noble, all-seeing Chenrezig, white, bright and radiating five-coloured light rays, smiling charmingly and gazing with eyes of compassion. He has four arms, the upper two joined together and the lower two holding a white lotus and a crystal rosary. He is adorned by precious jewels and silks; a deer skin covers his left shoulder. The Buddha of Boundless Light [Amitabha] adorns his head. He sits in the vajra asana; his back is supported by an immaculate moon; he is the essence of all sources of refuge.

While thinking that all beings are saying as if in a single voice, we pray:

"Lord, whose white body is not clothed by any fault, whose head is adorned by the Perfect Buddha, who looks upon all beings with the eyes of compassion, to you, Chenrezig, I pay homage. To the Sublime One, the Mighty Chenrezig, to the Buddhas and their sons, who reside in the ten directions and the three times, with complete sincerity I pay homage. I offer flowers, incense, butter-lamps, perfume, food, music and other real and imaginary offerings, and beseech the noble assembly to accept them. I confess all the harmful actions caused by the power of conflicting emotions, the ten un-virtuous deeds and the five sins of unlimited consequence done from beginningless time until now. I rejoice in the spiritual merit of whatever virtue *sravakas, pratyeka* Buddhas, bodhisattvas, and ordinary beings gather throughout the three times.

I pray that the dharma wheel of the Mahayana, Hinayana and of the teachings common to both be turned in accordance with the wishes and aptitudes of beings. I beseech the Buddhas not to pass into nirvana as long as the cycle of existences is not emptied, but to look with compassion upon sentient beings who wallow in the ocean of suffering. May whatever merit I have accumulated be the cause of enlightenment of beings; may I quickly acquire the qualities needed to be a saviour of beings. [...]

Wherever I am born, may my deeds, by equalling those of Chenrezig, liberate beings from impure realms and spread the perfect sound of the six syllables in the ten directions. Through the power of prayer to you, Perfect Noble One, may beings whom I am to discipline pay the greatest attention to action and result, and diligently practise virtue and the dharma for the benefit of beings.

Through this one-pointed prayer, light radiates from the body of the Sublime One and purifies impure karma, impure appearances, and the deluded mind. The outer reality is the Pure Land of Dewachen, and the body, speech and mind of beings, therein are the perfect form, sublime speech, and pure mind of Mighty Chenrezig, the invisible union of appearance, sound and vivid intelligence with voidness.

OM MANI PADME HUNG

My body, the body of others and all appearances are the perfect form of the Sublime One, all sounds the melody of the six syllables, all thoughts the vastness of the great supreme wisdom. Through this virtue, may I quickly achieve the realization of mighty Chenrezig and may I bring every single being to that same state. Through the merit of reciting this mantra and meditating, may I and every being to whom I am connected, when these imperfect forms are left behind, be miraculously born in *Dewachen*. May I then immediately cross the ten levels and send out emanations in the ten directions for the benefit of others. Through this virtue, may all beings perfect the accumulations of spiritual merit and awareness. May they attain the two supreme bodies which arise from merit and awareness. Bodhicitta is precious; may it arise in those who have not cultivated it. In those who have cultivated it, may it not diminish; may it ever grow and flourish."

Chenrezig Puja

> *May the compassion of Lord Chenrezig*
> *fill my heart and*
> *may this compassion fulfil itself*
> *in the liberation of all sentient beings.*

THE TRIANGLE OF LOVE

WE may represent love as a triangle, each of the angles of which corresponds to one of its inseparable characteristics. There can be no triangle without all its three angles; and there can be no true love without its three following characteristics.

The first angle of our triangle is that love knows no bargaining. Wherever there is any seeking for something in return, there can be no real love; it becomes a mere matter of shopkeeping. As long as there is in us any idea of deriving this or that favour from God in return for our respect and allegiance to him, so long there can be no true love growing in our hearts. Those who worship God because they wish him to bestow favours on them are sure not to worship him if those favours are not forthcoming. The bhakta loves the Lord because he is lovable; there is no other motive originating or directing this divine emotion of the true devotee. [...] Begging is not the language of love. To worship God even for the sake of salvation or any other rewards is equally degenerate. Love knows no reward. Love is always for love's sake. The bhakta loves because he cannot help loving. [...] Ask not anything in return for your love; let your position be always that of the giver; give your love unto God, but do not ask anything in return even from him.

The second angle of the triangle of love is that love knows no fear. Those that love God through fear are the lowest of human beings, quite undeveloped as men. They worship God from fear of punishment. He is a great Being to them, with a whip in one hand and the sceptre in the other; if they do not obey him, they are afraid they will be whipped. It is a degradation to worship God through fear of punishment; such worship is, if worship at all, the crudest form of the worship of love. So long as there is any fear in the heart, how can there be love also? Love conquers naturally all fear. [...] Fear comes from the selfish idea of cutting one's self off from the universe. The smaller and more selfish I make myself, the more is my fear. If a man thinks he is a little nothing, fear will surely come upon him. And the less you think of yourself as an insignificant person, the less fear there will be for you. So long as there is the least spark of fear in you there can be no love there. Love and fear are incompatible; God is never to be feared by those who love him. [...]

The third angle of the love-triangle is that love knows no rival, for in it is always embodied the lover's highest ideal. True love never comes until the object of our love becomes to us our highest ideal. It may be that in many cases human love is misdirected and mis-placed, but to the person who loves, the thing he loves is always his own highest ideal. One may see his ideal in the vilest of beings, and another in the highest of beings; nevertheless in every case it is the ideal alone that can be truly and intensely loved. The highest ideal of every man is called God. Ignorant or wise, saint or sinner, man or woman, educated or uneducated, cultivated or uncultivated, to every human being the highest ideal is God. The synthesis of all the high-est ideals of beauty, of sublimity, and of power gives us the com-pletest conception of the loving and lovable God. [...]

What is the ideal of the lover who has quite passed beyond the idea of selfishness, of bartering and bargaining, and who knows no fear? Even to the great God such a man will say, "I will give you my all, and I do not want anything from you; indeed there is nothing that I can call my own." When a man has acquired this conviction, his ideal becomes one of perfect love, one of the perfect fearlessness of love. The highest ideal of such a person has no narrowness of par-ticularity about it; it is love universal, love without limits and bonds, love itself, absolute love. This grand ideal of the religion of love is worshipped and loved absolutely as such without the aid of any symbols or suggestions. This is the highest form of *para-bhakti* – the worship of such an all-comprehending ideal as the ideal; all the other forms of bhakti are only stages on the way to reach it.

All our failures and all our successes in following the religion of love are on the road to the realisation of that one ideal. Object after object is taken up, and the inner ideal is successively projected on them all; and all such external objects are found inadequate as expo-nents of the ever-expanding inner ideal and are naturally rejected one after another. At last the aspirant begins to think that it is vain to try to realise the ideal in external objects, that all external objects are as nothing when compared with the ideal itself; and, in the course of time, he acquires the power of realising the highest and the most generalised abstract ideal entirely as an abstraction that is to him quite alive and real. When the devotee has reached this point, he is no more impelled to ask whether God can be demonstrated or not, whether he is omnipotent and omniscient or not. To him he is only the God of love; he is the highest ideal of love, and that is sufficient for all his purposes. He, as love, is self-evident. It requires no proofs to demonstrate the existence of the beloved to the lover. The magistrate-Gods of other forms of religion may require a great deal of proof to prove them, but the bhakta does not and cannot think of such Gods at all. To him God exists entirely as love. [...]

When this highest ideal of love is reached, philosophy is thrown away; who will then care for it? Freedom, salvation, nirvana – all are thrown away; who cares to become free while in the enjoyment of divine love? "Lord, I do not want wealth, nor friends, nor beauty, nor learning, nor even freedom; let me be born again and again, and be thou ever my love. Be thou ever and ever my love." [...] Who will then desire to become free and one with God? "I may know that I am he; yet will I take myself away from him and become different, so that I may enjoy the Beloved." That is what the bhakta says. Love for love's sake is his highest enjoyment. Who will not be bound hand and foot a thousand times over to enjoy the Beloved? No bhakta cares for anything except love, except to love and to be loved. His unworldly love is like the tide rushing up the river; this lover goes up the river against the current. The world calls him mad. [...] The true bhakta's love is this burning madness before which everything else vanishes for him. The whole universe is to him full of love and love alone; that is how it seems to the lover. So when a man has this love in him, he becomes eternally blessed, eternally happy. This blessed madness of divine love alone can cure for ever the disease of the world that is in us. With desire, selfishness has vanished. He has drawn near to God, he has thrown off all those vain desires of which he was full before.

We have all to begin as dualists in the religion of love. God is to us a separate being, and we feel ourselves to be separate beings also. Love then comes in the middle, and man begins to approach God, and God also comes nearer and nearer to man. Man takes up all the various relationships of life, as father, as mother, as son, as friend, as master, as lover, and projects them on his ideal of love, on his God. To him God exists as all these, and the last point of his progress is reached when he feels that he has become absolutely merged in the object of his worship. We all begin with love for ourselves, and the unfair claims of the little self make even love selfish. At last, however, comes the full blaze of light, in which this little self is seen to have become one with the infinite. Man himself is transfigured in the presence of this light of love, and he realises at last the beautiful and inspiring truth that Love, the Lover and the Beloved are One.

Swami Vivekananda, *Bhakti-Yoga*

True love of God knows no desire of gifts,
nor any fear;
God is the highest ideal of the devotee,
consumed and lost in love of God.

LOVE ONE ANOTHER

BELOVED, let us love one another, because love is of God; everyone who loves is born of God and knows God. Whoever does not love does not know God, for God is love. God's love was revealed among us in this way: God sent his only Son into the world so that we might live through him. In this is love, not that we loved God but that he loved us and sent his Son to be the atoning sacrifice for our sins. Beloved, since God loved us so much, we also ought to love one another. No one has ever seen God; if we love one another, God lives in us, and his love is perfected in us.

By this we know that we abide in him and he in us, because he has given us of his Spirit. And we have seen and do testify that the Father has sent his Son as the saviour of the world. God abides in those who confess that Jesus is the Son of God, and they abide in love. So we have known and believe the love that God has for us.

God is love, and those who abide in love abide in God, and God abides in them. Love has been perfected among us in this: that we have boldness on the day of judgement, because as he is, so are we in this world. There is no fear in love, but perfect love casts out fear, for fear has to do with punishment, and whoever fears has not reached perfection in love. We love because he first loved us. Those who say, "I love God," and hate their brothers or sisters, are liars; for those who do not love a brother or sister whom they have seen, cannot love God whom they have not seen. The commandment we have from him is this: those who love God must love their brothers and sisters also.

First Epistle of Saint John, 4

God is love:
may I repose in the love of God,
and love my fellows
as God loves me.

THE LESSON OF LOVE

THE PRIMARY lesson to learn in life is to love. Love is so strong that it is unbreakable, and yet it is intangible. You can know it; you can feel it; and yet you cannot hold onto it; for as soon as you try, it will slip away like quicksilver. Love cannot be possessed; it is as free as the wind and moves where it will. Move with it. Love is unity and wholeness. Love knows no limitation, no barriers. With love comes freedom. It is fear that binds and limits a soul; it is love that frees and cuts away all bonds. Love opens all doors, changes lives and melts the hardest of hearts. Love is creative; it builds up, creating beauty, harmony and oneness. It works for, not against, anything. Love brings such joy that it cannot be repressed. It dances and sings through life. Is there love in your heart? Love for each other? It starts in you and works out and out.

Eileen Caddy, *Opening Doors Within* (16 November)

> *Love is the essence of life;*
> *it unifies and frees,*
> *and brings joy and beauty to life.*

UNSELFISH LOVE

TRUE happiness is found in unselfish love, a love which increases in proportion as it is shared. There is no end to the sharing of love, and, therefore, the potential happiness of such love is without limit. Infinite sharing is the law of God's inner life. He has made the sharing of ourselves the law of our own being, so that it is in loving others that we best love ourselves. In disinterested activity we best fulfil our own capacities to act and to be.

Yet there can never be happiness in compulsion. It is not enough for love to be shared: it must be shared freely. That is to say, it must be given, not merely taken. Unselfish love that is poured out upon a selfish object does not bring perfect happiness: not because love requires a return or a reward for loving, but because it rests in the happiness of the beloved. And if the one loved receives love selfishly, the lover is not satisfied. He sees that his love has failed to make the beloved happy. It has not awakened his capacity for unselfish love.

Hence the paradox that unselfish love cannot rest perfectly except in a love that is perfectly reciprocated: because it knows that the only true peace is found in selfless love. Selfless love consents to be loved selflessly for the sake of the beloved. In so doing, it perfects itself.

The gift of love is the gift of the power and the capacity to love, and, therefore, to give love with full effect is also to receive it. So, love can only be kept by being given away, and it can only be given perfectly when it is also received. [...]

To love others well we must first love the truth. And since love is a matter of practical and concrete human relations, the truth we must love when we love our brothers is not mere abstract speculation: it is the moral truth that is to be embodied and given life in our own destiny and theirs. This truth is more than the cold perception of an obligation, flowing from moral precepts. The truth we must love in loving our brothers is the concrete destiny and sanctity that are willed for them by the love of God. One who really loves another is not merely moved by the desire to see him contented and healthy and prosperous in this world. Love cannot be satisfied with anything so incomplete. If I am to love my brother, I must somehow enter deep into the mystery of God's love for him. I must be moved not only by human sympathy but by that divine sympathy which is revealed to us in Jesus and which enriches our own lives by the outpouring of the Holy Spirit in our hearts.

The truth I love in loving my brother cannot be something merely philosophical and abstract. It must be at the same time supernatural and concrete, practical and alive. And I mean these words in no metaphorical sense. The truth I must love in my brother is God himself, living in him. I must seek the life of the Spirit of God breathing in him. And I can only discern and follow that mysterious life by the action of the same Holy Spirit living and acting in the depths of my own heart.

Thomas Merton, *No Man Is an Island*

> *Love can be preserved*
> *only by being given away:*
> *the fulfilment of love is the*
> *happiness of the beloved.*

THE ALTRUISTIC MIND

SHANTIDEVA says in his *Engaging in the Bodhisattva Deeds*:

Although sentient beings want to get rid of suffering,
They manifestly run to suffering itself.
Though they want happiness, out of confusion
They destroy their own happiness like an enemy.

Though people do not want suffering, they rush toward it; though
they want happiness, out of confusion they achieve the opposite.

To help sentient beings achieve liberation, we need to help them
to understand the techniques for achieving happiness and removing
suffering through identifying without error what to adopt and what
to discard. [...] In order fully to bring about the welfare of other sentient beings it is necessary to know from a subtle level those things
that will help others, the essential points of what to adopt and what
to discard. Beyond this, we need to know the dispositions, interests,
and so forth of the sentient beings you seek to help. Thus, it is necessary to remove the obstructions to knowing all objects of knowledge. For, when all these obstructions have been removed, one has
achieved the omniscience of a Buddha, the exalted wisdom knowing
all aspects of objects of knowledge.

Since bodhisattvas are seeking to help all sentient beings, they
take as their main object of abandonment the obstructions to omniscience and work at the antidote to these obstructions. For, without
knowing all, it is possible to help a small number of beings but
impossible fully and effectively to help a vast number. This is why
it is necessary to achieve Buddhahood in order to be of effective service to sentient beings.

Unable to bear the suffering of sentient beings without doing
something about it, you generate strong compassion and love, wishing beings to be rid of suffering and to possess happiness. Then, seeing that to accomplish this purpose there is no way but to achieve
Buddhahood, you generate the altruistic intention to achieve enlightenment. This intention to yourself attain the omniscience of a
Buddha in order to be of service to others is called the altruistic mind
of enlightenment (*bodhicitta*). It involves two aspirations – seeking

the welfare of others through seeking your own enlightenment. [...] If, no matter what you are doing, in some portion of the mind there remains a constant intense wish for the welfare of sentient beings and a seeking of enlightenment for their sake, you have generated a fully qualified altruistic mind of enlightenment. [...]

Having reached the point where a portion of the mind is continuously involved with the wish to achieve Buddhahood for the sake of all beings, you should conjoin this with the rite of aspirational mind generation for the sake of making it more stable. Also, it is necessary to train in the causes that will prevent deterioration of the aspirational mind in this or future lifetimes.

Then, it is not sufficient merely to generate the aspirational form of the mind of enlightenment; the practical mind of enlightenment must also be generated, for intention alone is not enough. You must come to understand that further training is necessary – the practice of the six perfections: giving, ethics, patience, effort, concentration and wisdom. Having trained in the wish to engage in these practices, you take the bodhisattva vows actually to do so. [...]

The foundation of the altruistic mind of enlightenment is a good heart, a good mind, at all times. All of us can benefit from cultivating this; we should not get angry, fight, backbite, and so forth. When people engage in such activities, they do so for the sake of personal concerns but actually are only harming themselves. All of us need to do whatever we can to cultivate a good mind, a good heart. I am not just explaining this; I, too, am doing as much as I can to practise it. Everyone needs to do whatever is possible, for as much as we can practise this, so much will it help.

Tenzin Gyatso (Dalai Lama), *The Path to Enlightenment*

> *The supreme expression of love and compassion*
> *is the aspiration to achieve enlightenment*
> *to relieve the suffering of all sentient beings.*

INTIMATIONS OF DIVINE LOVE

A love perfect, whole,
And he in beauty comes;
Words thronging my soul
And my tongue is dumb.

Did you ever meet
Stranger joy and woe;
Athirst, and at my feet
The living waters flow.

* * *

He whom I love so well
Softly whispers a spell;
My heart is all distraught,
My mind is lost in thought.

What is the magic word
He is whispering, Lord,
That this thing is sown
Within my heart of stone?

* * *

Love came to me, and said
Against spirit and head
I should rebel,
And with him only dwell.

Time and anon
I came, and again was gone;
Now I am in love's heart
Ne'er to depart.

Thou art gone, my heart's delight;
Yet never shall depart
Thy image from my sight,
Thy love from my heart.

About the world I go,
That haply thou wilt come
In the end, and to me wilt show
My winding way home.

* * *

Love came and went again,
Like blood within my flesh and vein;
From self love sets me free
And with the Friend completed me.

Only remains my name;
My being's every particle.
The Friend took for his claim,
And so the Friend became my whole.

* * *

The moon of love tonight
Is full, and wondrous bright;
The lady of my delight
Looks down from the roof upon me.

Tonight, my heart, recall
Thy Maker, and prostrate fall,
For tonight, like the cup, is all
Sleep forbidden thee.

As the essence that is mine
To the all-pervading sea
Turneth, all my atoms shine
In sublime resplendency.

On the road of love, behold!
Like a candle I do blaze,
That one moment may enfold
All the moments of my days.

*   *   *

As I stood before
My fair love's door
Smiling, smiling she
Came forth to me.

Close, close she pressed
Me against her breast:
"My lover true,
Wise and godly, too!"

A moment's rapture with the Friend
If thou mayest spend,
A life of joy were thine, in this
Brief moment's bliss.

Beware; this moment do not waste,
If such thou hast;
Scarce shall this joy, in a life of pain,
Return again.

*   *   *

Lo, we come carrying wine
From the Friend of heart's desire,
The flame of love divine
That sets the soul afire.

Until the world shall end
No dreamer will ever dream
Such nights, as here we spend
To the dawn's returning gleam.

Jalal od-Din Rumi, *Ruba'iyat*

He who is Love calls us to love;
love is the most noble,
the most grandiose, the most perfect
of human aspirations and achievements.

TO DIE OF LOVE

I LIVE, yet no true life I know,
And, living thus expectantly,
I die because I do not die.

Since this new death-in-life I've known,
Estranged from self my life has been,
For now I live a life unseen:
The Lord has claimed me as his own.
My heart I gave him for his throne,
Whereon he wrote indelibly:
"I die because I do not die."

Within this prison-house divine,
Prison of love whereby I live,
My God himself to me doth give,
And liberate this heart of mine.
And, as with love I yearn and pine,
With God my prisoner, I sigh:
"I die because I do not die."

How tedious is this life below,
This exile, with its griefs and pains,
This dungeon and these cruel chains
In which the soul is forced to go!
Straining to leave this life of woe,
With anguish sharp and deep I cry:
"I die because I do not die."

How bitter our existence ere
We come at last the Lord to meet!
For, though the soul finds loving sweet,
The waiting-time is hard to bear.
Oh, from this leaden weight of care,
My God, relieve me speedily,
Who die because I do not die.

I only live because I know
That death's approach is very sure,
And hope is all the more secure
Since death and life together go.
O death, thou life-creator, lo!
I wait upon thee, come thou nigh:
I die because I do not die.

Consider, life, love's potency,
And cease to cause me grief and pain.
Reflect, I beg, that, thee to gain,
I first must lose thee utterly.
Then, death, come pleasantly to me.
Come softly: undismayed am I
Who die because I do not die.

That life, with life beyond recall,
Is truly life forevermore:
Until this present life be over
We cannot savour life at all.
So, death, retreat not at my call,
For life through death I can descry
Who die because I do not die.

O life, what service can I pay
Unto my God who lives in me
Save if I first abandon thee
That I may merit thee for aye.
I'd win thee dying day by day,
Such yearning for my Spouse have I,
Dying because I do not die.

Teresa of Avila, "Poems"

To love God is to die to oneself;
to die to oneself
is to achieve life eternal.

THE SHEPHERD

THE LORD is my shepherd; I shall not want.
He makes me lie down in green pastures;
  he leads me beside the still waters;
  he restores my soul.
He leads me in right paths
  for his name's sake.

Even though I walk through the darkest valley,
  I fear no evil;
  for you are with me;
  your rod and your staff –
  they comfort me.

You prepare a table before me
  in the presence of my enemies;
  you anoint my head with oil;
  my cup overflows.

Surely goodness and mercy shall follow me
  all the days of my life,
  and I shall dwell in the house of the Lord
  my whole life long.

Psalm 23

> *God is my guide*
> *and the recourse of my life;*
> *his love protects me from all evil*
> *and leads me to him.*

4 GOD IS WISDOM

THE WAY AND THE VIRTUE

THE WAY gives birth to all things,
Virtue fosters them,
Nature shapes them,
 each perfected according to its kind.
Therefore all creatures honour the Way
 and esteem Virtue,
Not by command, but by their own nature.

Therefore the Way gives all things life;
And Virtue nourishes them,
Develops and fosters them;
Harbours and comforts them.

Create, but do not possess;
Lead without mastering:
This is the mysterious Virtue.

Lao Tzu, *Tao Te Ching*, LI

> *The great way of the Eternal is to give life;*
> *the way of life is virtue;*
> *by which one returns to the Eternal.*

THE PERFECTION OF WISDOM

ADORATION to the Prajnaparamita, which is beyond words, thought and praise, whose self-nature is, like unto space, neither created nor destroyed, which is a state of wisdom and morality evident to our inner consciousness, and which is the mother of all Excellent Ones of the past, present and future.

Thus I heard. At one time the World-honoured One dwelt at Rajagriha, on Vulture Peak, together with a large number of bhikshus and bodhisattvas. At that time the World-honoured One was absorbed in a samadhi known as deep enlightenment. And at the same moment the great Bodhisattva Avalokiteshvara was practising himself in the deep prajnaparamita.

The great Bodhisattva Avalokiteshvara perceived that there are five *skandas* [form, sensation, thought, confection, consciousness]; and these he saw in their self-nature to be empty.

"O Sariputra, form is here emptiness, emptiness is form; form is no other than emptiness, emptiness is no other than form; that which is form is emptiness, and that which is emptiness is form. The same can be said of sensation, thought, confection and consciousness.

"O Sariputra, all things here are characterized with emptiness: they are not born, they are not annihilated; they are not tainted, they are not immaculate; they do not increase, they do not decrease. Therefore, O Sariputra, in emptiness there is no form, no sensation, no thought, no confection, no consciousness; no eye, ear, nose, tongue, body, mind; no form, sound, colour, taste, touch, objects; no *dhatu* [element] of vision, till we come to no dhatu of consciousness; there is no knowledge, no ignorance, till we come to there is no old age and death; there is no suffering, no accumulation, no annihilation, no path; there is no knowledge, no attainment, [and] no realization, because there is no attainment. In the mind of the bodhisattva who dwells depending on the prajnaparamita there are no obstacles; and, going beyond the perverted views, he reaches final nirvana. All the Buddhas of the past, present and future, depending on the prajnaparamita, attain the highest perfect enlightenment.

"Therefore, one ought to know that the prajnaparamita is the great mantra, the mantra of great wisdom, the highest mantra, the peerless mantra, which is capable of allaying all pain; it is truth because it is not falsehood: this is the great mantra proclaimed in the prajna-paramita. It runs:

Gate, gate, paragate, parasamgate, bodhi, svaha!

[O Bodhi, gone, gone, gone to the other shore,
landed at the other shore, Svaha!]

[Gone, gone, gone beyond, gone altogether beyond,
O what an awakening, all-hail!]

"O Sariputra, thus should the bodhisattva practise himself in the deep prajnaparamita."

At that moment, the World-honoured One rose from the samadhi and gave approval to the great Bodhisattva Avalokiteshvara, saying: "Well done, well done, noble son! so it is! so should the practice of deep prajnaparamita be carried on. As it has been preached by you, it is applauded by tathagatas and arhats."

Thus spoke the World-honoured One with a joyful heart. The venerable Sariputra and the great Bodhisattva Avalokiteshvara, together with the whole assemblage, and the world of gods, men, asuras and gandharvas [demi-gods and spirits], all praised the speech of the World-honoured One.

Prajnaparamita Sutra or Hannya Shingyo
(Heart Sutra Perfection of Wisdom Sutra)

All perceptions are illusory, without real existence;
only emptiness is without beginning and without end;
its realization is the great wisdom,
the finality of human existence.

GOD AND THE SOUL

"GOD is nearer to the soul than the soul is to itself" (St. Augustine).
My body is more in my soul than my soul is in my body but both
body and soul are more in God than they are in themselves and that
is justice, righteousness, and the prime cause of every thing. God
and the soul are so nearly related to each other that there is really no
distinction between them. By the same kind of knowledge by which
God knows himself, that is, detached or dispassionate knowledge,
the soul receives its being from God. For that reason God is closer
to the soul than the soul is to itself and therefore, God is the soul's
core – God and all the Godhead. [...]

The true archetype of the soul is revealed when God alone and
nothing else can be described or imagined. The soul has two eyes -
one looking inwards and the other outwards. It is the inner eye of the
soul that looks into essence and takes being directly from God. That
is its true function. The soul's outward eye is directed towards creatures and perceives their external forms but when a person turns
inwards and knows God in terms of his own awareness of him, in the
roots of his being, he is then freed from all creation and is secure in
the castle of truth. [...]

I have spoken of an agent in the soul whose primitive function it
is, not to reach God as he is good, or to apprehend him as he is the
truth, but to go further, to the foundations, to seek him and to apprehend him in his uniqueness and abstraction, in the desert of his solitude, the essence of his being. Still unsatisfied, it looks further to see
what he is in his Godhead and also looks to the most intimate properties of his nature. Now, they say that there is no unity more perfect
than that of the three persons in God. One might say further that
there is no unity more perfect than that between the soul and God.
When the soul is kissed by the Godhead, it is then completely perfected and blessed and embraced by the unity of God. When God
has touched the soul and rendered it uncreaturely, it is then as high
in rank as God himself, after he has touched it. Contemplating the
creature, God gives it being, and contemplating God, the creature
receives its being. The soul has an intelligent, knowing essence and
therefore, wherever God is, there is the soul, and wherever the soul
is, there is God!

There is an agent in the soul, untouched by time and flesh, which proceeds out of the Spirit and which remains forever in the Spirit and is completely spiritual. In this agent, God is perpetually verdant and flowering with all the joy and glory that is in him. Here is joy so hearty, such inconceivably great joy that no one can ever fully tell it, for in this agent the eternal Father is ceaselessly begetting his eternal Son and the agent is parturient with God's offspring and is itself the Son, by God's unique power. [...]

There is, however, still another agent, which also is not incarnate but which proceeds out of the Spirit, yet remains in it and is always only spiritual. In this second agent, God glows and burns without ceasing, in all his fullness, sweetness and rapture. Truly, it holds joy so great and rapture so unmeasured that no one can tell it or reveal it. Yet I say that if there were one person who could look into it for a moment and still keep his right mind, all he had ever suffered or that God wished him to suffer would be a very little thing indeed, nothing at all. Nay – I go ever further – suffering would be to him always a joy and pleasure. [...]

I have said that there is one agent in the soul that is free. Sometimes I have called it the tabernacle of the Spirit. Other times I have called it the light of the Spirit and again, a spark. Now I say that it is neither this nor that. It is something higher than this or that, as the sky is higher than the earth and I shall call it by a more aristocratic name than I have ever used before, even though it disowns my adulation and my name, being far beyond both. It is free of all names and unconscious of any kind of forms. It is at once pure and free, as God himself is, and like him is perfect unity and uniformity, so that there is no possible way to spy it out.

God blossoms and is verdant in this agent of which I speak, with all the Godhead and spirit of God and there he begets his only begotten Son as truly as if he were in himself. For he lives really in this agent, the Spirit together with the Father giving birth to the Son and in that light, he is the Son and the Truth.

Meister Eckhart, *Sermons*

> *The soul is blessed with a sacredness*
> *beyond all that we can conceive:*
> *the presence of God, its creator.*

THE FOUNTAIN OF LIFE

NOW hear, O son of Partha [Arjuna], how by practising *yoga* in full consciousness of me, with mind attached to me, you can know me in full, free from doubt. I shall now declare unto you in full this knowledge both phenomenal and noumenal, by knowing which there shall remain nothing further to be known. Out of many thousands among men, one may endeavour for perfection, and of those who have achieved perfection, hardly one knows me in truth.

Earth, water, fire, air, ether, mind, intelligence and false ego – all together these eight comprise my separated material energies. Besides this inferior nature, O mighty Arjuna, there is a superior energy of mine, which consists of all living entities who are struggling with material nature and who are sustaining the universe. Of all that is material and all that is spiritual in this world, know for certain that I am both the origin and dissolution. O conqueror of wealth, there is no truth superior to me. Everything rests upon me, as pearls are strung on a thread.

O son of Kunti, I am the taste of water, the light of the sun and the moon, the syllable OM in Vedic mantras; I am the sound in ether and ability in man. I am the original fragrance of the earth, and I am the light in fire. I am the life of all that lives, and I am the penances of all ascetics. Know that I am the original seed of all existences, the intelligence of the intelligent, and the prowess of all powerful men. I am the strength of the strong, devoid of passion and desire... All states of being – goodness, passion or ignorance – are manifested by my energy. I am, in one sense, everything – but I am independent. I am not under the modes of this material nature. Deluded by the three modes [goodness, passion and ignorance], the whole world does not know me, who am above them and inexhaustible. This divine energy of mine, consisting of the three modes of material nature, is difficult to overcome. But those who have surrendered unto me can easily cross beyond it.

Bhagavad Gita, 7

I am here; I am close to you;
I underlie all that exists on earth and in heaven:
know me therefore.

ONE SENSIBLE WORD

BETTER than a speech of a thousand meaningless words is one sensible word which brings peace to the hearer. Better than a poem of a thousand meaningless words is one verse of a hymn which brings peace to the hearer. Better than a hundred verses of senseless words is one stanza of the law which brings peace to the hearer.

If a man should conquer in battle a thousand times a thousand men, and another should conquer himself, he is the greatest of conquerors. Conquest of self is indeed greater than conquest of others. Not even a god, a *gandharva*, neither Mara nor Brahma could turn into defeat the victory of he who has vanquished himself and lives always with restraint.

Better than offering a thousand sacrifices month after month for a hundred years is a moment's homage to a man whose soul is grounded in true knowledge. Better than tending the sacrificial fire in the forest for a hundred years is a moment's homage to a man whose soul is grounded in true knowledge. Offerings or oblations made for a whole year to gain merit are not worth a quarter of reverence shown to the righteous. Four treasures will increase to those who always honour and revere the aged in virtue: long life, beauty, happiness and strength.

Better than an evil and unrestrained life of a hundred years is one day in virtue and contemplation. Better than a life of a hundred years in ignorance and licentiousness is one day in wisdom and contemplation. Better than a life of a hundred years in idleness and weakness is one day of courage and striving. Better than a life of a hundred years in ignorance of the beginning and the end of things is one day knowing the origin and finality of things.

Better than a life of a hundred years unawakened to immortality is one day contemplating immortality. Better than a life of a hundred years blind to the supreme law is one day aware of the supreme law.

Dhammapada, 8

*To know and accomplish and honour
the way of wisdom:
this is the greatest realization.*

THE FIRST AND THE LAST

GOD draws our attention to what is originated as an aid to knowledge of him and says [in the Koran] that he will show forth his signs in it. Thus he suggests that knowledge of him is inferred in knowledge of ourselves. Whenever we ascribe any quality to him, we are ourselves [representatives of] that quality, except it be the quality of his self-sufficient Being. Since we know him though ourselves and from ourselves, we attribute to him all we attribute to ourselves. It is for this reason that the divine revelations come to us through the mouths of interpreters, for he describes himself to us through us. If we witness him we witness ourselves, and when he sees us he looks on himself.

There is no doubt that we are, as individuals and types, many, and that, though representatives of a single reality, we know definitely that there is a factor distinguishing one individual from another, but for which, multiplicity would not be [implicit] in the One. In the same way, even if we describe ourselves as he describes himself, in all possible aspects, there would still remain an inevitable factor of distinction. This is our dependence on him for existence, which, in our case, derives entirely from him because we are originated while he is free of all dependence whatsoever. Thus is he rightly called the One without beginning, the Ancient of Days, contradicting all priority in the sense of existence starting from non-existence. For, although he is the First, no temporal priority may be attributed of him. Thus he is called also the Last. Even if he were the First in the sense of being the first-determined existence, he could not be called the Last in this sense, since contingent being has no end, being infinite. He is called the Last only in the sense that all reality, though reality be attributed to us, is his. His finality is essentially in his priority as is his priority essentially in his finality.

Know also that the Reality has described himself as being the Outer and the Inner. He brought the cosmos into being as constituting an unseen realm and a sensory realm, so that we might perceive the Inner through the unseen and the Outer through their sensory aspect.

He has also attributed of himself pleasure and wrath, having created the cosmos as [expressing] both fear and hope, fear of his wrath and hope for his pleasure. He has also described himself as being possessed of beauty and majesty, having created us as combining awe and intimacy, and so on with all his attributes and names. He has expressed this polarity of qualities as being his hands devoted to the creation of the perfect man who integrates in himself all cosmic realities and their individual [manifestations].

Ibn Al-Arabi, *The Bezels of Wisdom*

God is the One, the First and the Last:
we can know him through the manifest universe,
and through ourselves: the source and
perfection of human qualities.

THE MIDDLE PATH

THUS have I heard. The Blessed One was once living in the Deer Park at Isipatana near Baranasi (Benares). There he addressed the group of five bhikkus:

"Bhikkus, these two extremes ought not to be practised by one who has gone forth from the household life. What are the two? There is devotion to the indulgence of the sense-pleasures, which is low, common, the way of ordinary people, unworthy and unprofitable; and there is devotion to self-mortification, which is painful, unworthy and unprofitable.

"Avoiding both these extremes, the Tathagata has realized the middle path: it gives vision, it gives knowledge, and it leads to calm, to insight, to enlightenment, to *nibbana*. And what is that middle path...? It is simply the noble eightfold path, namely, right view, right thought, right speech, right action, right livelihood, right effort, right mindfulness, right concentration. This is the middle path realized by the Tathagata, which gives vision, which gives knowledge, and which leads to calm, to insight, to enlightenment, to *nibbana*.

"The noble truth of suffering is this: birth is suffering; aging is suffering; sickness is suffering; death is suffering; sorrow and lamentation, pain, grief and despair are suffering; association with the unpleasant is suffering; dissociation from the pleasant is suffering; not to get what one wants is suffering – in brief, the five aggregates of attachment are suffering.

"The noble truth of the origin of suffering is this: it is this thirst (craving) which produces re-existence and re-becoming, bound up with passionate greed. It finds fresh delight now here and now there, namely, thirst for sense-pleasures; thirst for existence and becoming; and thirst for non-existence (self-annihilation).

"The noble truth of the cessation of suffering is this: it is the complete cessation of that very thirst, giving it up, renouncing it, emancipating oneself from it, detaching oneself from it.

"The noble truth of the path leading to the cessation of suffering is this: it is simply the noble eightfold path, namely right view, right thought, right speech, right action, right livelihood, right effort, right mindfulness, right concentration. [...]

"As long as my vision of true knowledge was not fully clear...

regarding the four noble truths, I did not claim to have realized the perfect enlightenment that is supreme in the world with its gods, with its Maras and Brahmas, in this world with its recluses and brahmanas, with its princes and men. But when my vision of true knowledge was fully clear ... regarding the four noble truths, then I claimed to have realized the perfect enlightenment that is supreme in the world with its gods, its Maras and Brahmas, in this world with its recluses and brahmanas, with its princes and men.

"And a vision of true knowledge arose in me thus: my heart's deliverance is unassailable. This is the last birth. Now there is no more re-becoming (rebirth)."

This the Blessed One said. The group of five bhikkus was glad, and they rejoiced at his words.

Dhammacakkappavattana Sutta
(The First Sermon of the Buddha)

> *The middle way lies between the extremes*
> *of sensual pleasures and excessive privation;*
> *it is the way of the cessation of suffering,*
> *supreme knowledge and final illumination.*

THE WHEEL OF CREATION

BY the yoga of meditation and contemplation the wise saw the power of God, hidden in his own creation. It is he who rules over all the sources of this universe, from time to the soul of man.

And they saw the wheel of his power made of one circle, three layers, sixteen parts, fifty spokes, twenty counterspokes, six groups of eight, three paths, one rope of innumerable strands, and the great illusion: which sees the ONE as two.

They also saw the river of life impetuously rushing with the five streams of sense-feelings which come from the five sources, the five elements. Its waves are moved by five breathing winds, and its origin is a fivefold fountain of consciousness.

This river has five whirlpools, and the violent waves of five sorrows. It has five stages of pain and five dangerous windings and turnings.

In this vast wheel of creation wherein all things live and die, wanders around the human soul like a swan in restless flying, and she thinks that God is afar. But when the love of God comes down upon her, then she finds her own immortal life.

Exalted in songs has been Brahman. In him are God and the world and the soul, and he is the imperishable supporter of all. When the seers of Brahman see him in all creation, they find peace in Brahman and are free from all sorrows.

God upholds the oneness of this universe: the seen and the unseen, the transient and the eternal. The soul of man is bound by pleasure and pain; but when she sees God she is free from all fetters.

There is the soul of man with wisdom and unwisdom, power and powerlessness; there is nature, *prakriti*, which is creation for the sake of the soul; and there is God, infinite, omnipresent, who watches the work of creation. When a man knows the three he knows Brahman.

Matter in time passes away, but God is for ever in eternity, and he rules both matter and soul. By meditation on him, by contemplation of him, and by communion with him, there comes in the end the destruction of earthly delusion.

When a man knows God, he is free: his sorrows have an end, and birth and death are no more. When in inner union he is beyond the

world of the body, then the third world, the world of the Spirit, is
found, where the power of the All is, and man has all: for he is one
with the ONE.

Svetasvatara Upanishad, I

Wise is he who sees beyond
the visible universe, constantly in flux,
and who attains knowledge of the unchangeable,
the immortal, the Brahman.

THE WISDOM OF THE WALKER

WHERE are we going, along this road we have been following for so
long without once asking where it leads? Some have taken it to seek
fortune, some to drive away care, some to seek out knowledge, and
some in order to go home. We are going to do all these things at the
same time: we are going to return to the obvious.

$*\quad*\quad*$

He who walks has not arrived. The pilgrim is not a wise man, he
is not a saint; he is a friend of wisdom and a seeker after saintliness.
The truth you are looking for is not at the end of the road. It is everywhere: it is in you. It is yourself you are looking for, you madman,
and here you go running to fetch yourself from afar.

Yes, my body dragging in the outer world still does not know the
truth my intelligence has seen. I want to put my feet into the foot-
prints of my thought, I want to feel with my hands what my knowledge knows, I want to weigh my weight on the promised land of
spiritual certainty. Go on then, you fool! Start walking with all your
life. Let the road take the dried reed of your body and the wind your
legs and teach them to sing.

$*\quad*\quad*$

If you close your hand, the world will remain closed to you like a
fist. If you want the world to open up to you, open your hand first.

$*\quad*\quad*$

Endeavour to do what nobody but you can do. Endeavour to want
what everybody else can have as well. Distinguish yourself by what
you are, not by what you have.

$*\quad*\quad*$

Pray, friend, in the early hours tuneful with dew drops and clear
trills. The mist that rises in the rising light will carry up your voice.
If you pray to ask, do not ask to receive, ask to purify desire. Pray
God rather to purify you of all desire. Yes, do not pray in order to
ask, but pray to give thanks and sing glory. Pray to take part in the
growth of the trees, in the leaves in the wind, in the birds in the light,
in the work of the illustrious planets, in the ecstasy of the stars forever established in truth.

You know that you are. That is the first self-evidence. But the knowledge of what you are is knowledge of which all knowledge is ignorant. How can you see him who hides behind your own eyes?

* * *

Be silent much in order to have something to say worth hearing. But again be silent to hear yourself. Silence is the rind of fruit without which everything dries up before autumn.

* * *

If you speak of your love, you love with your lips only. If you speak of your sacrifices, the approval of your listeners seems less vain to you than deliverance and wisdom. If you speak of your visions, others will not see them, and you will soon cease to see them yourself... If you speak of the most precious thing you have, the only thing that belongs to you, of the good you have done, it is sold: you have your reward in words.

* * *

No word is equal to the thought. No thought is equal to the truth. The word brings surfaces closer. Thought is built with words. Truth dwells in the abyss. That man alone dwells in truth who is silent and, through wisdom, has ceased to think.

* * *

To contemplate is to achieve truth without discovering it, without seeing it from the outside, without revealing it with words. In contemplation, man forgets himself, thought forgets that it thinks, the object shines itself, thinks by itself. Higher still, man attends his own absence. He sees the effacement of every object. The nothing that remains is a presence that suffices for everything. The light that reigns there has no limits of object. The joy that reigns there has no reason, no limits of reason.

Lanza del Vasto, *The Return to the Obvious*

*The pilgrim is a seeker,
a seeker of truth, of wisdom, of himself;
he will find the goal of his quest
only within himself.*

THE TRUE SELF

THE SELF alone exists and is real. The world, the individual and God are, like the illusory appearance of silver in the mother-of-pearl, imaginary creations in the Self. They appear and disappear simultaneously. Actually, the Self alone is the world, the "I" and God. All that exists is only a manifestation of the Supreme.

*   *   *

Reality must always be real. It has no names or forms but is what underlies them. It underlies all limitations, being itself limitless. It is not bound in any way. It underlies unrealities, being itself Real. It is that which is. It is as it is. It transcends speech and is beyond description such as being or non-being.

*   *   *

The names and forms which constitute the world continually change and perish and are therefore called unreal. It is unreal (imaginary) to limit the Self to these names and forms and real to regard all as the Self. The non-dualist says that the world is unreal, but he also says, "All this is Brahman." So it is clear that what he condemns is regarding the world as objectively real in itself, not regarding it as Brahman. He who sees the Self sees the Self alone in the world also. It is immaterial to the enlightened whether the world appears or not. In either case, his attention is turned to the Self.

*   *   *

The individual being which identifies its existence with that of the life in the physical body as "I" is called the ego. The Self, which is pure Consciousness, has no ego-sense about it. Neither can the physical body, which is inert in itself, have this ego-sense. Between the two, that is between the Self or pure Consciousness and the inert physical body, there arises mysteriously the ego-sense or "I" notion, the hybrid which is neither of them, and this flourishes as an individual being. This ego or individual being is at the root of all that is futile and undesirable in life. Therefore it is to be destroyed by any possible means; then that which ever is alone remains resplendent. This is liberation or enlightenment or self-realization.

Everyone is the Self and, indeed, is infinite. Yet each person mistakes his body for his Self. In order to know anything, illumination is necessary. This can only be of the nature of light; however, it lights up both physical light and physical darkness. That is to say, that it lies beyond apparent light and darkness. It is itself neither, but is said to be light because it illuminates both. It is infinite and is Consciousness. Consciousness is the Self of which everyone is aware. No one is ever away from his Self and therefore everyone is in fact Self-realized; only – and this is the great mystery – people do not know this and want to realize the Self. Realization consists only in getting rid of the false idea that one is not realized. It is not anything new to be acquired. It must already exist or it would not be eternal and only what is eternal is worth striving for.

Once the false notion "I am the body" or "I am not realized" has been removed, Supreme Consciousness or the Self alone remains and in people's present state of knowledge they call this "Realization". But the truth is that Realization is eternal and already exists, here and now.

* * *

Consciousness is pure knowledge. The mind arises out of it and is made up of thoughts.

* * *

The Self alone is real. All else is unreal. The mind and intellect have no existence apart from you. The Bible says: "Be still and know that I am God." Stillness is the only thing needed to realize that I am is God.

The Teachings of Ramana Maharshi

The True Self alone is real;
silence beyond words and thought:
it is always present,
just as I am always realized.

SEEDS OF FREEDOM

EVERY moment and every event of every man's life on earth plants something in his soul. For just as the wind carries thousands of winged seeds, so each moment brings with it germs of spiritual vitality that come to rest imperceptibly in the minds and hearts of men. Most of these unnumbered seeds perish and are lost, because men are not prepared to receive them: for such seeds as these cannot spring up anywhere except in the good soil of freedom, spontaneity and love.

This is not new idea. Christ in the parable of the sower long ago told us that "The seed is the word of God." [...] Every expression of the will of God is in some sense a "word" of God and therefore a "seed" of new life. The ever-changing reality in the midst of which we live should awaken us to the possibility of an uninterrupted dialogue with God..., a dialogue of love and of choice. A dialogue of deep wills.

In all the situations of life the "will of God" comes to us not merely as an external dictate of impersonal law but above all as an interior invitation of personal love. [...] We must learn to realize that the love of God seeks us in every situation, and seeks our good. His inscrutable love seeks our awakening. True, since this awakening implies a kind of death to our exterior self, we will dread his coming in proportion as we are identified with this exterior self and attached to it. But when we understand the dialectic of life and death we will learn to take the risks implied by faith, to make the choices that deliver us from our routine self and open to us the door of a new being, a new reality.

The mind that is the prisoner of conventional ideas, and the will that is the captive of its own desire cannot accept the seeds of an unfamiliar truth and a supernatural desire. For how can I receive the seeds of freedom if I am in love with slavery and how can I cherish the desire of God if I am filled with another and an opposite desire? God cannot plant his liberty in me because I am a prisoner and I do not even desire to be free. I love my captivity and I imprison myself in the desire for the things that I hate, and I have hardened my heart against true love. I must learn therefore to let go of the familiar and the usual and consent to what is new and unknown to me. I must learn to "leave myself" in order to find myself by yielding to the love of God. If I were looking for God, every event and every moment would sow, in my will, grains of his life that would spring up one day in tremendous harvest.

For it is God's love that warms me in the sun and God's love that sends the cold rain. It is God's love that feeds me in the bread I eat and God that feeds me also by hunger and fasting. It is the love of God that sends the winter days when I am cold and sick, and the hot summer when I labour and my clothes are full of sweat: but it is God who breathes on me with light winds off the river and in the breezes out of the wood. [...] It is God's love that speaks to me in the birds and streams; but also behind the clamour of the city God speaks to me in his judgements, and all these things are seeds sent to me from his will.

If these seeds would take root in my liberty, and if his will would grow from my freedom, I would become the love that he is, and my harvest would be his glory and my own joy. [...]

In all that happens, my one desire and my one joy should be to know: "Here is the thing that God has willed for me. In this his love is found, and in accepting this I can give back his love to him and give myself with it to him. For in giving myself I shall find him and he is life everlasting."

By consenting to his will with joy and doing it with gladness I have his love in my heart, because my will is now the same as his love and I am on the way to becoming what he is, who is love. And by accepting all things from him I receive his joy into my soul, not because things are what they are but because God is who he is, and his love has willed my joy in them all.

Thomas Merton, *New Seeds of Contemplation*

> *The seeds that God plants in my life*
> *are the events of every day:*
> *accepting them as his love for me,*
> *I grow in freedom, joy and love.*

THE SPIRIT OF WISDOM

WISDOM is radiant and unfading,
   and she is easily discerned by those who love her,
   and is found by those who seek her.
She hastens to make herself known
   to those who desire her.
One who rises early to seek her
   will have no difficulty,
   for she will be found sitting at the gate.
To fix one's thought on her is perfect understanding,
   and one who is vigilant on her account
   will soon be free from care,
because she goes about seeking those worthy of her,
   and she graciously appears to them in their paths,
   and meets them in every thought.

The beginning of wisdom is the most sincere
   desire for instruction,
   and concern for instruction is love of her,
   and love of her is the keeping of her laws,
   and giving heed to her laws is assurance of immortality,
   and immortality brings one near to God;
so the desire for wisdom leads to a kingdom. [...]

There is in her a spirit
   that is intelligent, holy,
   unique, manifold, subtle,
   mobile, clear, unpolluted,
   distinct, invulnerable, loving the good,
   keen, irresistible, beneficent,
   humane, steadfast, sure,
   free from anxiety, all-powerful,
   overseeing all, and penetrating through all spirits
   that are intelligent, pure, and altogether subtle.
For wisdom is more mobile than any motion;
   because of her pureness
   she pervades and penetrates all things.

For she is a breath of the power of God,
  and a pure emanation of the glory of the Almighty;
  therefore nothing defiled gains entrance into her.
For she is a reflection of eternal light,
  a spotless mirror of the working of God,
  and an image of his goodness.
Although she is but one,
  she can do all things,
and while remaining in herself,
  she renews all things;
in every generation she passes into holy souls
  and makes them friends of God, and prophets;
for God loves nothing so much as
  the person who lives with wisdom.

The Wisdom of Solomon, 6-7

---

*Wisdom is the manifestation
of the power and goodness of God:
a reflection of the eternal light
which dissipates the darkness of evil.*

DARE TO SAY YES

EVERY human being dreams of perfect happiness and a life in which there would be only joy. Until then, we seek pleasant emotions and reject painful ones. But the key to liberation, the great teaching, consists in abandoning this way of thinking. That which all traditions and all religions call "beatitude", "felicity", "everlasting joy", "plenitude", cannot be and is not the triumph of the happiness which we know over the suffering which we know. There are no positive emotions without negative ones; suffering is but the other face of happiness. [...]

The *sadhaka* [he who seeks truth] puts all emotions in the same bag. For a person can only be freed from suffering by also being freed from pleasure. If he renounces one, he must also renounce the other. If he desires one, he must desire the other in the same way. The *sadhaka* must consider all emotions as emotions, as manifestations of the prison in which he is enclosed. The Path only really commences on the day on which the disciple begins to accept suffering as well as joy, without wanting to destroy them. [...] One must accept the unacceptable, from the moment that it is upon us, the terror, the suffering, the anguish, everything that makes us say: "I can't take any more, I don't want any more", while thinking: "The spiritual life or yoga will free me of these." Yes, the Path will free you. This has been its promise to humanity across the centuries and the millennia: "I will lead you beyond all suffering." But it will liberate you only if you accept pain and suffering completely, as completely as you accept the positive emotions, the beautiful ones, the grandiose emotions, those which cause us to say that "life is nonetheless worth living". [...]

We are asked to give completely and without second thought the right to exist of everything that manifests itself, of everything that appears in us, even the worst, the most unacceptable, the most agonizing. Not to have this outlook is to harbour a subtle wish to kill. This suffering, be it "moral" or "physical", is there. I cannot dispose of it at will, get rid of it, like my watch, my jacket or my shoes. Consequently I do not have the right to say that I am not this suffering. If I *have* pain, I can dispose of it: but this I cannot do. Hence I *do not have* pain, I *am* the pain in question, at this moment. If at the moment that I am aware of my suffering, I reject it, I am saying yes and no at the same time. No, there should not be pain. I am not who I am. And this is what is dramatic. This simultaneous yes and no creates a duality which can also be expressed as me *and* my pain. But truth is always, in all circumstances, non-dual. All the striving of the *sadhaka* must consist in becoming one with this pain, until there is no more pain: "suffering is perceived" and not "I perceive suffering": the "I" has disappeared. [...]

The Path of the peace which surpasses all understanding comprises the acceptance of the natural play of the emotions without any reservation: not to strive to prolong positive emotions and no longer to want to cut off prematurely intolerable emotions. Oh, I know that this is not easy and especially that it does not seem easy to say yes to a fear or an agony which we reject with all our being. The help of a master, the presence of this help, is indispensable to convince us that the unacceptable must be accepted. Only a profound sense of submission to the divine will suffices for the person who really has the attitude of the young child towards Providence.

Every emotion must be greeted as an expression in us of the universal revelation, of the unique infinite energy. I accept fully that this joy will not last and I accept fully that this suffering is there. I allow each one to evolve as they will. I am one with them. If I want my happiness to last, it means that there is "I" *and* my happiness. If I want my suffering to cease, it means that there is "I" *and* my suffering. By adhering to my suffering, by turning away from the no which arises in me and which is a lie because it denies what is, by finding strength on the contrary in what is, in my agony, to say yes, YES, YES, sooner or later comes the moment when the acceptance is so complete that duality disappears: I am my emotion. There is no longer anyone to suffer. And, at that exact moment, suffering vanishes completely and gives way to peace.

Arnaud Desjardins, *Les Chemins de la Sagesse*

I am my joys; I am my sorrows:
by accepting myself completely, I die to myself,
in order to reach the peace of my essential self.

TRUTH IS A PATHLESS LAND

TRUTH is a pathless land, and you cannot approach it by any path whatsoever, by any religion, by any sect... Truth, being limitless, unconditioned, unapproachable by any path whatsoever, cannot be organized; nor should any organization be formed to lead or coerce people along any particular path. If you first understand that, then you will see how impossible it is to organize a belief. A belief is purely an individual matter, and you cannot and must not organize it. If you do, it becomes dead, crystallized; it becomes a creed, a sect, a religion, to be imposed on others. This is what everyone throughout the world is attempting to do. Truth is narrowed down and made a plaything for those who are weak, for those who are only momentarily discontented. Truth cannot be brought down, rather the individual must make the effort to ascend to it. You cannot bring the mountain-top to the valley. If you would attain to the mountain-top you must pass through the valley, climb the steeps, unafraid of the dangerous precipices. You must climb towards the Truth, it cannot be "stepped down" or organized for you. Interest in ideas is mainly sustained by organizations, but organizations only awaken interest from without. [...]

No organization can lead man to spirituality. If an organization be created for this purpose, it becomes a crutch, a weakness, a bondage, and must cripple the individual, and prevent him from growing, from establishing his uniqueness, which lies in the discovery for himself of that absolute, unconditioned Truth. [...]

The only spirituality is the incorruptibility of the self which is eternal, is the harmony between reason and love. This is the absolute, unconditioned Truth which is Life itself. I want therefore to set man free, rejoicing as the bird in the clear sky, unburdened, independent, ecstatic in that freedom... Truth is in everyone; it is not far, it is not near; it is eternally there.

Jiddu Krishnamurti, "The Dissolution of the Order of the Star"

> *Truth lies within;*
> *and I alone know the path*
> *which leads me to this Truth.*

LIBERATION AND LOVE

MAN being free, is wholly responsible to himself, unguided by any plan, by any spiritual authority, by any divine dispensation whatsoever. As he is free, he is, by that very freedom, limited. If you were not free, you would have a different world from that which exists at present. As the will in everyone is free, it is limited, and because the self is small, without determination or purpose at the beginning, it chooses, it discriminates, has its likes and has its dislikes. In the removal of that limitation, which is self-imposed on the self, lies the glory of the fulfilment of the self, the freedom of the self.

There must be a removal of the barriers imposed on the self by the self, a constant breaking down of limitations, till the self arrives at that condition, where no more barriers exist between it and the eternal. Such a state, which is limitless, immeasurable, is liberation. It is the self, made incorruptible. Perfection of the self is immortality. Wherever is imperfection, wherever is limitation, there is sorrow; and man is constantly seeking a way, consciously or unconsciously, by which he can arrive at that perfection which will give him ineffable serenity, calmness, pliability of the mind, the assuredness of incorruptible love. That is what man is seeking by constant effort; that is what you are all seeking. You are trying to establish within yourselves that harmony which cannot be disturbed either by loneliness or by companionship, either by sorrow and pain or by ecstasy and great rejoicing. You are seeking that freedom which will make you absolutely serene, untouched by the opposites. The "I"-ness in the self, which causes barriers around you, which separates and segregates, which creates false realities, must be made pure and incorruptible.

Jiddu Krishnamurti, *Now*

> *The Self strives to attain liberation:*
> *liberation which is incorruptibility and love*
> *and is the perfection of life.*

THAT THOU ART

JUST as every jar and vessel made of earth is held to be earth only, so all this, born of Being, having Being as its essence, is Being only, since there is nothing beyond Being; in truth, "This is the Real, this is the Self," therefore, "That thou art", the Eternal, full of peace, pure, undivided, supreme.

As in a dream, the imagined space and time and objects and perceiver are all unreal, so also here in waking, the world is conjured up by our unwisdom; since this body, its powers and life-breath, and the thought of it as "I" are all unreal, therefore, "That thou art", the Eternal, full of peace, pure, undivided, supreme.

That Eternal, which transcends birth and rule and race and clan, having nor name nor form nor quality nor fault, dwelling beyond space and time and all things objective, "That thou art"; bring it to consciousness in thy Self.

That Eternal, which cannot be attained by any speech, yet is attained by the pure vision of illumination, a realm of pure consciousness, beginningless substance, "That thou art"; bring it to consciousness in thy Self.

That Eternal, which rises above the six waves of human weakness [pain, delusion, age, death, hunger, thirst], which dwells in the heart of him who has attained to union, which cannot be discerned by thy powers or known by thy understanding, flawless, "That thou art"; bring it to consciousness in thy Self.

That Eternal, which, self-supported, is the support of the world built up through illusion, which is other than the existent or the nonexistent, partless, which can be reached by no similitude, "That thou art"; bring it to consciousness in thy Self.

That Eternal, which is free from birth and growth and change, waning and sickness and death, everlasting, the cause that puts forth, upholds, destroys the world, "That thou art"; bring it to consciousness in thy Self.

That Eternal, wherein all difference ceases, whose character never changes, still as a waveless ocean, for ever free, in nature impartite, "That thou art"; bring it to consciousness in thy Self.

That Eternal, which, being One, is the cause of many, the cause that sets aside all other causes, itself apart from cause and what is caused, "That thou art"; bring it to consciousness in thy Self.

That Eternal, which is unchanging, mighty, imperishable, other than that which perishes and that which perishes not, supreme, everlasting, eternal joy, stainless, "That thou art"; bring it to consciousness in thy Self.

That Eternal, the one which appears manifold, through illusion, through change of name and form and character, itself changeless like the gold in many ornaments, "That thou art"; bring it to consciousness in thy Self.

That Eternal, which shines alone, beyond the highest, hidden, of single essence, of the character of the supreme Self, eternal substance, wisdom, joy, endless, everlasting, "That thou art"; bring it to consciousness in thy Self.

Shankaracharya, *Vivekachudamani*
(*The Crest-Jewel of Discrimination*)

> *I bring to consciousness in my Self*
> *that imperishable Eternal:*
> *purity, peace, wisdom, joy:*
> *I am that, and no other.*

EQUANIMITY AND DETACHMENT

AS long as I am seated in this meditation,
  I shall patiently suffer all calamities
  that may befall me, be they caused by an animal,
  a human being, or a god.

I renounce, for the duration [of this meditation],
  my body, all food, and all passions.
Attachment, aversion, fear, sorrow, joy,
  anxiety, self-pity...all these
  I abandon with body, mind, and speech.
I further renounce all delight and
  all repulsion of a sexual nature.

Whether it is life or death, whether gain or loss,
  whether defeat or victory, whether meeting or separation,
  whether friend or enemy, whether pleasure or pain,
I have equanimity towards all.

In [the attainment of] knowledge, insight,
  and proper conduct,
  [the cause] is invariably nothing but my own soul.

Similarly, my soul [is the primary cause] for both
  the influx of karmas and the stopping of that influx.

Once and eternal is my soul,
  characterized by intuition and knowledge;
All other states that I undergo are external to me,
  for they are formed by associations.

Because of these associations
  my soul has suffered the chains of misery;
Therefore I renounce with body, mind, and speech,
  all relationships based on such associations.

Thus have I attained to equanimity
and to my own self-nature.
May this state of equanimity be with me
until I attain to salvation.

Nityanaimittika-pathavali (Jaina)

*Through renunciation and detachment
from all the fluctuations of life
I can attain to equanimity:
the realization of my essential nature.*

WISDOM AND SIMPLICITY

ABBOT Pambo questioned Abbot Anthony saying: What ought I to do? And the elder replied: Have no confidence in your own virtuousness. Do not worry about a thing once it has been done. Control your tongue and your belly.

*   *   *

Someone inquired of Father Abbot Nisteros the great, the friend of Abbot Anthony, asking: What good work shall I do? He replied: Not all works are alike. For Scripture says that Abraham was hospitable and God was with him. Elias loved solitary prayer, and God was with him. And David was humble, and God was with him. Therefore, whatever you see your soul to desire according to God, do that thing, and you shall keep your heart safe.

*   *   *

Abbot Arsenius, when he was still in the King's palace, prayed to the Lord saying: Lord, lead me to salvation. And a voice came to him saying: Arsenius, fly from men and you shall be saved. Again, embracing the monastic life, he prayed in the same words. And he heard a voice saying to him: Arsenius, fly, be silent, rest in prayer: these are the roots of non-sinning.

*   *   *

A certain brother went to Abbot Moses in Scete, and asked him for a good word. And the elder said to him: Go, sit in your cell, and your cell will teach you everything.

*   *   *

A certain brother inquired of Abbot Pastor, saying: What shall I do? I lose my nerve when I am sitting alone at prayer in my cell. The elder said to him: Despise no one, condemn no one, rebuke no one, God will give you peace and your meditation will be undisturbed.

*   *   *

A brother came to Abbot Pastor and said: Many distracting thoughts come into my mind, and I am in danger because of them. Then the elder thrust him into the open air and said: Open up the garments about your chest and catch the wind in them. But he replied: This I cannot do. So the elder said to him: If you cannot catch the wind, neither can you prevent distracting thoughts from coming into your head. Your job is to say No to them.

One of the monks, called Serapion, sold his book of the Gospels and gave the money to those who were hungry, saying: I have sold the book which told me to sell all that I had and give to the poor.

* * *

One of the brethren had sinned, and the priest told him to leave the community. So then Abbot Bessarion got up and walked out with him, saying: I too am a sinner!

* * *

The same Father said: If there are three monks living together, of whom one remains silent in prayer at all times, and another is ailing and gives thanks for it, and the third waits on them both with sincere good will, these three are equal, as if they were performing the same work.

* * *

A certain elder said: Apply yourself to silence, have no vain thoughts, and be intent in your meditation, whether you sit at prayer, or whether you rise up to work in the fear of God. If you do these things, you will not have to fear the attacks of the evil ones.

* * *

One of the Fathers said: Just as it is impossible for a man to see his face in troubled water, so too the soul, unless it be cleansed of alien thoughts, cannot pray to God in contemplation.

* * *

Abbot Pastor said: Any trial whatever that comes to you can be conquered by silence.

Thomas Merton, *The Wisdom of the Desert*

> *To accomplish the will of God:*
> *this is the most important;*
> *in simplicity, silence and humility,*
> *each must find his path to God.*

REASON AND PASSION

YOUR soul is oftentimes a battlefield, upon which your reason and your judgement wage war against your passion and your appetite.

Would that I could be a peacemaker in your soul, that I might turn the discord and the rivalry of your elements into oneness and melody. But how shall I, unless you yourselves be also the peacemakers, nay, the lovers of all your elements?

Your reason and your passion are the rudder and the sails of your seafaring soul.

If either your sails or your rudder be broken, you can but toss and drift, or else be held at a standstill in mid-seas. For reason, ruling alone, is a force confining; and passion, unattended, is a flame that burns to its own destruction.

Therefore let your soul exalt your reason to the height of passion, that it may sing; and let it direct your passion with reason, that your passion may live through its own daily resurrection, and like the phoenix rise above its own ashes.

I would have you consider your judgement and your appetite even as you would two loved guests in your house. Surely you would not honour one guest above the other; for he who is more mindful of one loses the love and the faith of both.

Among the hills, when you sit in the cool shade of the white poplars, sharing the peace and serenity of distant fields and meadows – then let your heart say in silence, "God rests in reason."

And when the storm comes, and the mighty wind shakes the forest, and thunder and lightning proclaim the majesty of the sky, – then let your heart say in awe, "God moves in passion."

And since you are a breath in God's sphere, and a leaf in God's forest, you too should rest in reason and move in passion.

Kahlil Gibran, *The Prophet*

> *I am both reason and passion:*
> *my reason leads me to just decisions,*
> *and my passion engages me on the way of truth.*

5   GOD IS JOY

I AND THOU

BLESSED time! when we were sitting, I and thou,
With two forms and only one soul, I and thou.
Fragrance, song of birds, they quicken ev'rything
When we come into the garden, I and thou.

All the stars of heaven hurry to see us
And we show them our own moon, I and thou -
I and thou without words, without I and thou -
In delight we are united, I and thou.

Sugar chew the heaven's parrots in that place
Where we're sitting, laughing sweetly, I and thou.
Strange that I and thou together in this nook
Are apart a thousand miles, see – I and thou.
One form in this dust, the other in that land,
Sweet eternal paradise there...
        I and thou.

Jalal od-Din Rumi, *Divan-i-Shams-i-Tabriz*

The quiet joy of love:
it bridges the gulf separating man from God:
eternal wonder and delight.

THE BLESSED

BLESSED are the poor in spirit,
  for theirs is the kingdom of heaven.
Blessed are those who mourn,
  for they will be comforted.
Blessed are the meek,
  for they will inherit the earth.
Blessed are those who hunger and thirst for righteousness,
  for they will be filled.
Blessed are the merciful,
  for they will receive mercy.
Blessed are the pure in heart,
  for they will see God.
Blessed are the peacemakers,
  for they will be called children of God.
Blessed are those who are persecuted for
    the righteousness' sake,
  for theirs is the kingdom of heaven.

Blessed are you when people revile you and persecute you and utter all kinds of evil against you falsely on my account. Rejoice and be glad, for your reward is great in heaven, for in the same way they persecuted the prophets who were before you.

You are the salt of the earth; but if the salt has lost its taste, how can its saltiness be restored? It is no longer good for anything, but is thrown out and trampled under foot.

You are the light of the world. A city built on a hill cannot be hid. No one after lighting a lamp puts it under the bushel basket, but on the lampstand, and it gives light to all in the house. In the same way, let your light shine before others, so that they may see your good works and give glory to your Father in heaven.

The Gospel According to Matthew, 5

> *Blessed are those who follow*
> *the ways of the divine;*
> *the kingdom of heaven is truly theirs.*

THE UNIVERSE IS AFLAME

WHEN your presence, Lord, has flooded me with its light I hoped that within it I might find ultimate reality at its most tangible.

But now that I have in fact laid hold on you, you who are utter consistency, and feel myself borne by you, I realize that my deepest hidden desire was not to possess you but to be possessed.

It is not as a radiation of light nor as subtilized matter that I desire you; nor was it thus that I described you in my first intuitive encounter with you: it was as fire. And I can see I shall have no rest unless an active influence, coming forth from you, bears down on me to transform me.

The whole universe is aflame.

Let the starry immensities therefore expand into an ever more prodigious repository of assembled suns;

let the light-rays prolong indefinitely, at each end of the spectrum, the range of their hues and their penetrative power;

let life draw from yet more distant sources the sap which flows through its innumerable branches;

and let us go on and on endlessly increasing our perception of the hidden powers that slumber, and the infinitesimally tiny ones that swarm about us, and the immensities that escape us because they appear to us simply as a point.

From all these discoveries, each of which plunges him a little deeper into the ocean of energy, the mystic derives an alloyed delight, and his thirst for them is unquenchable; for he will never feel himself sufficiently dominated by the powers of the earth and the skies to be brought under God's yoke as completely as he would wish.

It is in fact God, God alone, who through his Spirit stirs up into a ferment the mass of the universe.

Pierre Teilhard de Chardin, *Pensées (Le Milieu Mystique)*

---

*God manifests himself in the splendours
and mysteries of the visible universe,
aflame with the divine presence.*

COMMUNION WITH INFINITE JOY

THE IMMORTAL *being manifests himself in joy-form.* His manifestation in creation is out of his fullness of joy. It is the nature of this abounding joy to realize itself in form which is law. The joy, which is without form, must create, must translate itself into forms. The joy of the singer is expressed in the form of a song, that of the poet ·in the form of a poem. Man in his role of a creator is ever creating forms, and they come out of his abounding joy.

This joy, whose other name is love, must by its very nature have duality for its realization. When the singer has his inspiration he makes himself into two; he has within him his other self as the hearer, and the outside audience is merely an extension of this other self of his. The lover seeks his own other self in his beloved. It is the joy that creates this separation, in order to raise through obstacles the union.

The *amritam*, the immortal bliss, has made himself into two. Our soul is the loved one, it is his other self. [...] Yes, our individual soul has been separated from the supreme soul, but this has not been from alienation but from the fullness of love. It is for that reason that untruths, sufferings, and evils are not at a standstill; the human soul can defy them, can overcome them, nay, can altogether transform them into new power and beauty.

The singer is translating his song into singing, his joy into forms, and the hearer has to translate back the singing into the original joy; then the communion between the singer and the hearer is complete. The infinite joy is manifesting itself in manifold forms, taking upon itself the bondage of law, and we fulfil our destiny when we go back from forms to joy, from law to the love, when we untie the knot of the finite and hark back to the infinite.

The human soul is on its journey from the law to love, from discipline to liberation, from the moral plane to the spiritual. Buddha preached the discipline of self-restraint and moral life; it is a complete acceptance of law. But this bondage of law cannot be an end by itself; by mastering it thoroughly we acquire the means of getting beyond it. It is going back to Brahman, to the infinite love, which is manifesting itself through the finite forms of law.

Buddha names it *Brahma-vihara*, the joy of living in Brahman.
[...]

For love is the ultimate meaning of everything around us. It is not a mere sentiment; it is truth; it is the joy that is at the root of all creation. It is the white light of pure consciousness that emanates from Brahman. So, to be one with this *sarvanubhuh*, this all-feeling being who is in the external sky, as well as in our inner soul, we must attain to that summit of consciousness, which is love: *Who could have breathed or moved if the sky were not filled with joy, with love?* It is through the heightening of our consciousness into love, and extending it over all the world, that we can attain *Brahma-vihara*, communion with this infinite joy.

Rabindranath Tagore, *Sadhana*

> *God created me to manifest*
> *his infinite love, his infinite joy;*
> *through love and joy*
> *I achieve oneness with him.*

THE JOY OF DIVINE LOVE

LORD God, holy lover of my soul, when you come into my heart, all that is within me rejoices. You are my glory and the joy of my heart; you are my hope and my refuge in the time of tribulation.

As I am yet weak in love and imperfect in virtue, I have great need of your strength and comfort; visit me often, therefore, I pray, and instruct me in all holy discipline. Set me free from evil passions, and heal my heart of all inordinate affections; that, inwardly cured and thoroughly cleansed, I may be fit to love, courageous to suffer and steadfast to persevere.

Love is a great thing, a mighty and thorough good; love alone makes all that is heavy, light, and all that is uneven, smooth. It bears every burden as no burden, and makes all that is bitter, sweet and savoury. The noble love of Jesus impels us to do great things and stirs us always to long for what is more perfect. Love aspires to loftiness and will not be restrained by anything base. Love desires to be free, liberated from worldly affections, lest its inner sight be hindered, or it be entangled in worldly prosperity, or subdued by adversity.

Nothing is sweeter than love, nothing stronger, nothing higher, nothing wider, nothing more pleasant, nothing fuller nor better in heaven or earth; because love is born of God, and cannot rest but in God, above all created things.

Those who love, fly, run, and rejoice; they are free and unbound. They give all for all and possess all in all, resting in One who is highest above all things, from whom all that is good flows and proceeds. They do not look upon the gifts, but elevate themselves to the Giver. Often love knows no limits, but is fervent beyond measure.

Love feels no burden, thinks nothing of affliction, attempts things beyond its strength; never pleads that anything is impossible; for it considers all things possible and all things permissible. Love is therefore able to undertake all things; and it completes and perfects many, while those who lack love faint and lie down. Love is watchful; resting, it never sleeps; fatigued, it is never exhausted; bound, it is never restrained; alarmed, it is never confounded: but like a living flame and a burning torch, it surges upward and serenely triumphs over every obstacle.

Whoever loves knows well the cry of this voice. For it is a loud cry in the ears of God, that ardent affection of the soul which exclaims "My God, my love, you are all mine, and I am all yours!"

Deepen your love in me, that I may taste in the depths of my heart how sweet it is to love, and to be dissolved, and to bathe myself in your love. Let me be possessed by love and rise above myself, in an excess of fervour and amazement. Let me sing the song of love. Let me follow you, my beloved, to the heights of your glory. Let my soul consume itself in your praise, rejoicing for love. Let me love you more than myself, and myself only for your own sake; and in you may I love all who truly love you, as the law of love commands, radiating from you.

Love is dynamic, sincere, affectionate, pleasant and amiable; love is courageous, patient, faithful, prudent, long-suffering, vigorous, and never self-seeking. For whoever is self-seeking abandons love. Love is vigilant, humble, and upright; love is not fickle or sentimental or attendant to vanities. Love is sober, pure, steadfast, quiet, and guarded in all the senses. Love is compliant and obedient to its superiors, mean and contemptible to itself, devoted and thankful to God, trusting and hoping always in him, even when he does not bestow his sweetness; for none can live in love without sorrow.

Thomas à Kempis, *The Imitation of Christ*, III

What great joy is the love of God!
He who truly loves is carried beyond himself;
he lives in the sweetness and the light of love.

THE PURE LAND

I AM a happy man, indeed!
I visit the Pure Land as often as I like:
I'm there and I'm back,
I'm there and I'm back,
I'm there and I'm back,
"Namu-amida-butsu!¹ Namu-amida-butsu!"

*   *   *

How happy I am!
"Namu-amida-butsu!"
I am the Land of Bliss,
I am Oya-sama.¹
"Namu-amida-butsu! Namu-amida-butsu!"

*   *   *

O Saichi, where is your land of bliss?
My Land of Bliss is right here.
Where is the line of division
Between this world and the land of bliss?
The eye is the line of division.

*   *   *

How grateful I feel!
Everything I do in this world -
My daily work for livelihood -
This is all transferred into building up the Pure Land.

*   *   *

I work in this world in company with all Buddhas,
I work in this world in company with all bodhisattvas;
Protected by Oya-sama I am here;
I know many who have preceded me along this path.
I am sporting in the midst of the *Namu-amida-butsu.*
How happy I am with the favour!
"Namu-amida-butsu!"

---

¹ *"Namu-amida-butsu"* (Japanese): "Adoration to the Buddha of Infinite Light" (*Amida or Amita: Amitabha* in Sanskrit). *Oya-sama*: an honorific title for Amida. *Nyorai: tathagata* in Sanskrit.

O Saichi, I am the most fortunate person!
I am altogether free from woes of all kind,
Not at all troubled with anything of the world.
Nor do I even recite the *"Namu-amida-butsu"*!
I'm saved by your mercifulness, O Amida-san!
How pleased I am with your favour!
"Namu-amida-butsu!"

*   *   *

The Oya-sama who never fails me
Has now become myself,
Making me hear his name -
The *"Namu-amida-butsu."*

*   *   *

I am a fortunate one:
Oya-sama is given me,
The Oya who turns me into a Buddha -
"Namu-amida-butsu!"

*   *   *

Oya is in the Pure Land,
I am in this world,
And Oya has given me,
To become one with me:
The *"Namu-amida-butsu"*!

*   *   *

Amida is this: "See, here I am!"
Namu and Amida -
They make out the *"Namu-amida-butsu."*
O Nyorai-san[1], such things I write,
How happy!

Saichi, *Journals*

> *Happiness, the Land of Bliss,*
> *is where I am right now:*
> *I have all I need to be one*
> *with the One in the Pure Land.*

OCEAN OF NECTAR

OCEAN of nectar, full of grace,
  engulfing the universe in your splendour!
O Arunachala, the supreme Itself!
Be you the sun and open
  the lotus of my heart in bliss!

O Arunachala! in you the picture
  of the universe is formed,
  has its stay and is dissolved;
  this is the sublime truth.
You are the inner self,
  who dances in the heart as "I".
Heart is your name, O Lord!

He who turns inward with untroubled mind
  to search where the consciousness of "I" arises,
  realizes the Self,
  and rests in you, O Arunachala!
  like a river when it joins the ocean.

Abandoning the outer world
  with mind and breath controlled,
  to meditate on you within,
  the yogi sees your light, O Arunachala!
  and finds his delight in you.

He who dedicates his mind to you and,
  seeing you, always beholds the universe
  as your figure,
  he who at all times glorifies you and loves you
  as none other than the Self,
  he is the master without rival,
  being one with you, O Arunachala!
  and lost in your bliss.

Ramana Maharshi, "Sri Arunachala Pancharatna"

> *True joy is found in the realization*
> *of the Supreme Self,*
> *which flourishes in the inner depths of the self,*
> *the lotus of the heart.*

THE GLORY OF GOD

I KNOW the Spirit supreme, radiant like the sun beyond darkness. He who knows him goes beyond death, for his is the only path to life immortal. His infinity is beyond what is great or small, and greater than him there is nothing. Like a tree everlasting he stands in the centre of heaven, and his radiance illumines all creation. Those who know him who is greater than all, beyond form and beyond pain, attain immortality; those who know not go to the worlds of sorrow.

All this universe is in the glory of God, of Siva the god of love. The heads and faces of men are his own and he is in the hearts of all. He is indeed the Lord supreme whose grace moves the hearts of men. He leads us unto his own joy and to the glory of his light. He is the inmost soul of all, which like a little flame the size of a thumb is hidden in the hearts of men. He is the master of wisdom ever reached by thought and love. He is the immortality of those who know him.

God is in truth the whole universe: what was, what is, and what beyond shall ever be. He is the god of life immortal, and all life that lives by food. The light of consciousness comes to him through infinite powers of perception, yet he is above these powers. He is God, the ruler of all, the infinite refuge of all.

Without hands he holds all things, without feet he runs everywhere. Without eyes he sees all things, without ears all things he hears. He knows all, but no one knows him, the Spirit before the beginning, the Spirit Supreme everlasting.

Concealed in the heart of all beings lies the Atman, the Spirit, the Self; smaller than the smallest atom, greater than the greatest spaces. When by the grace of God man sees the glory of God, he sees him beyond the world of desire and then sorrows are left behind.

I know that Spirit whose infinity is in all, who is ever one beyond time. I know the Spirit whom the lovers of Brahman call eternal, beyond the birth and rebirth of life.

Svetasvatara Upanishad, III

> *I know the Spirit Supreme,*
> *brilliant like the sun beyond the darkness,*
> *finer than the finest, greater than the greatest;*
> *those who know him achieve immortality.*

JOY IN HEAVEN

NOW all the tax collectors and sinners were coming near to listen to him. And the Pharisees and the scribes were grumbling and saying, "This fellow welcomes sinners and eats with them."

So he told them this parable: "Which one of you, having a hundred sheep and losing one of them, does not leave the ninety-nine in the wilderness and go after the one that is lost until he finds it? When he has found it, he lays it on his shoulders and rejoices. And when he comes home, he calls together his friends and neighbours, saying to them: 'Rejoice with me, for I have found my sheep that was lost.' Just so, I tell you, there will be more joy in heaven over one sinner who repents than over ninety-nine righteous persons who need no repentance.

"Or what woman having ten silver coins, if she loses one of them, does not light a lamp, sweep the house, and search carefully until she finds it? When she has found it, she calls together her friends and neighbours, saying, 'Rejoice with me, for I have found the coin that I had lost.' Just so, I tell you, there is joy in the presence of the angels of God over one sinner who repents."

Then Jesus said, "There was a man who had two sons. The younger of them said to his father, 'Father, give me the share of the property that will belong to me.' So he divided his property between them. A few days later the younger son gathered all he had and travelled to a distant country, and there he squandered his property in dissolute living. When he had spent everything, a severe famine took place throughout that country, and he began to be in need. So he went and hired himself out to one of the citizens of that country, who sent him to the fields to feed the pigs. He would gladly have filled himself with the pods that the pigs were eating; and no one gave him anything. But when he came to himself and said, 'How many of my father's hired hands have bread enough and to spare, but here am I dying of hunger! I will get up and go to my father, and I will say to him, "Father, I have sinned against heaven and before you; I am no longer worthy to be called your son; treat me like one of your hired hands." '

"So he set off and went to his father. But while he was still far off, his father saw him and was filled with compassion; he ran and put his arms around him and kissed him. Then the son said to him, 'Father, I have sinned against heaven and before you; I am no longer worthy to be called your son.' But the father said to his slaves, 'Quickly, bring out a robe – the best one – and put it on him; put a ring on his finger and sandals on his feet. And get the fatted calf and kill it, and let us eat and celebrate; for this son of mine was dead and is alive again; he was lost and is found!' And they began to celebrate.

The Gospel According to Luke, 15

Embarking on the spiritual path,
at whatever stage in one's life,
is always a cause of great joy.

JOY AND TRUTH

THE SATYAGRAHA Ashram owes its very existence to the pursuit and attempted practice of truth. The word *satya* is derived from *sat*, which means that which is. *Satya* means a state of being. Nothing is or exists in reality except truth. That is why *sat* or *satya* is the right name for God. In fact it is more correct to say that Truth is God than to say that God is Truth. But as we cannot do without a ruler or general, the name God is and will remain more current. On deeper thinking, however, it will be realized that *sat* or *satya* is the only correct and fully significant name for God.

And where there is truth, there is also knowledge which is true. Where there is no truth, there can be no true knowledge. That is why the word *chit* or knowledge is associated with the name of God. And where there is true knowledge, there is always *ananda*, bliss. There sorrow has no place. And even as truth is eternal, so is the bliss derived from it. Hence we know God as *sat-chit-ananda*, one who combines in himself truth, knowledge, and bliss.

Devotion to this truth is the sole justification for our existence. All our activities should be centred in truth. Truth should be the very breath of our life. When once this stage in the pilgrim's progress is reached, all other rules of correct living will come without effort and obedience to them will be instinctive. But without truth it is impossible to observe any principles or rules in life. [...]

The path of truth is as narrow as it is straight. Even so is that of *ahimsa* [non-violence]. It is like balancing oneself on the edge of a sword. By concentration an acrobat can walk on a rope. But the concentration required to tread the path of truth and *ahimsa* is far greater. The slightest inattention brings one tumbling to the ground. One can realize truth and *ahimsa* only by ceaseless striving.

But it is impossible for us to realize perfect truth as long as we are imprisoned in this mortal frame. We can only visualize it in our imagination. We cannot, through the instrumentality of this ephemeral body, see face to face truth which is eternal. That is why in the last resort we must depend on faith.

It appears that the impossibility of the full realization of truth in this mortal body led some ancient seeker after truth to the appreciation of *ahimsa*. The question which confronted him was: "Shall I bear with those who create difficulties for me, or shall I destroy them?" The seeker realized that he who went on destroying others did not make headway but simply stayed where he was, while the man who suffered those who created difficulties marched ahead and at times even took the others with him. The first act of destruction taught him that the truth which was the object of his quest was not outside himself but within. Hence the more he took to violence, the more he receded from truth. For in fighting the imagined enemy without, he neglected the enemy within. [...]

Without *ahimsa* it is not possible to seek after and find truth. *Ahimsa* and truth are so intertwined that it is practically impossible to disentangle and separate them. They are like the two sides of a coin, or rather of a smooth unstamped metallic disc. Who can say which is the obverse and which is the reverse? Nevertheless, *ahimsa* is the means and truth is the end. Means to be means must always be within our reach, and so *ahimsa* becomes our supreme duty and truth becomes God for us. If we take care of the means, we are bound to reach the end sooner or later. If we resolve to do this, we shall have won the battle. Whatever difficulties we encounter, whatever apparent reverses we sustain, we should not lose faith but should ever repeat one mantra: "Truth exists, it alone exists. It is the only God and there is but one way of realizing it; there is but one means and that is *ahimsa*. I will never give it up. May the God that is truth, in whose name I have taken this pledge, give me the strength to keep it."

Mohandas Gandhi, "Letters to the Ashram, 1930"

God is truth, because he alone is;
through ahimsa, *non-violence, true love,*
I attain to his truth, knowledge and bliss.

JOYOUS ENERGY

THE PARAMITA of energy, *virya*, is the kind of energy that immediately leads us into situations so that we never miss a chance, never miss an opportunity. In other words, it is joy, joyous energy... This energy is joy, rather than the kind of energy with which we work hard because we feel we must. It is joyous energy because we are completely interested in the creative patterns of our lives. One's whole life is opened by generosity, activated by morality, strengthened by patience, and now one arrives at the next stage, that of joy. One never sees situations as uninteresting or stagnant at all, because the bodhisattva's view of life is extremely open-minded, intensely interested. He never evaluates; though that does not mean that he becomes a complete blank. It does not mean that he is absorbed into a "higher consciousness", the "highest state of samadhi", so that he cannot differentiate day from night or breakfast from lunch. It does not mean that he becomes vague or woolly-minded. Rather, he actually sees verbalized and conceptualized values as they are, and then he sees beyond concept and evaluation. He sees the sameness of these little distinctions that we make. He sees situations from a panoramic point of view and therefore takes a great deal of interest in life as it is. So the bodhisattva does not strive at all; he just lives.

He takes a vow when he enters the bodhisattva path that he will not attain enlightenment until he has helped all sentient beings to attain the awakened state of mind or buddhahood before him. Beginning with such a noble act of giving, of opening, of sacrifice, he continues to follow this path, taking tremendous interest in everyday situations, never tired of working with life. This is *virya*, working hard with joy. There is tremendous energy in realizing that we have given up trying to become the Buddha, that now we have the time to really live life, that we have gone beyond neurotic speed.

Interestingly, although the bodhisattva has taken a vow not to attain enlightenment, because he is so precise and accurate, he never wastes one second. He always lives life thoroughly and fully, and the result is that, before he realizes where he is, he has attained enlightenment. But his unwillingness to attain enlightenment continues, strangely enough, even after he has reached Buddhahood. Then compassion and wisdom really burst out, reinforcing his energy and conviction. If we never tire of situations, our energy is joyous. If we are completely open, fully awake to life, there is never a dull moment. This is *virya*.

Chögyam Trungpa, *Cutting Through Spiritual Materialism*

> *The desire to work for the liberation*
> *of all sentient beings,*
> *produces a marvellous energy,*
> *and the joyful accomplishment of one's task.*

THE SUPREME GOOD

THE VERITABLY pleasant lies away in that other realm, the most to be loved and sought for, not something brought about and changing but the very principle of all the colour and radiance and brightness found here... We achieve the truly desirable by leading ourselves up to what is best within us; this best is what is symmetry, beauty, collective Idea, life clear, intellective, and good. [...]

Lovers here mould themselves to the beloved; they seek to increase their attraction of the person and their likeness of mind; they are unwilling to fall short in moral quality or in other graces lest they be distasteful to those possessing such merit – and only among such can true love be. In the same way the soul loves the Supreme Good, from its very beginnings stirred by it to love. The soul which has never strayed from this love waits for no reminding from the beauty of our world: holding that love – perhaps unawares – it is ever in quest, and, in its longing to be borne thither, passes over what is lovely here and with one glance at the beauty of the universe dismisses all. [...]

No longer can we wonder that the Principle evoking such longing should be utterly free from shape, even shape intellectual. The very soul, once it has conceived the straining love towards this, lays aside all the shape it has taken, even to the intellectual shape that has informed it. There is no vision, no union, for those handling or acting by anything other; the soul must see before it neither evil nor good nor anything else, that alone it may receive the Alone.

Suppose the soul to have attained: the highest has come to her, or rather has revealed its presence; she has turned away from all about her and made herself apt, beautiful to the utmost, brought into likeness with the divine – by those preparings and adornings which come unbidden to those growing ready for the vision. She has seen that presence suddenly manifesting within her, for there is nothing between: here is no longer a duality but a two in one; for, so long as the presence holds, all distinction fades: it is as lover and beloved here, in a copy of that union, long to blend; the soul has now no further awareness of being in body and will give herself no foreign name, not man, not living being, not being, not all. Any observation of such things falls away; the soul has neither time nor taste for

them; This she sought and This she has found and on This she looks
and not upon herself; and who she is that looks she has not leisure
to know.

Once there she will barter for This nothing the universe holds; not
though one would make over the heavens entire to her; than This
there is nothing higher, nothing of more good; above This there is no
passing; all the rest however lofty lies on the downgoing path: she is
of perfect judgement and knows that This was her quest, that nothing higher is. Here can be no deceit; where could she come upon
truer than the truth? and the truth she affirms, that she is herself; but
all the affirmation is later and is silent. In this happiness she knows
beyond delusion that she is happy; for this is no affirmation of an
excited body but of a soul become again what she was in time of her
early joy. All that she had welcomed of old – office, power, wealth,
beauty, knowledge – of all she tells her scorn as she never could had
she not found their better; linked to This she can fear no disaster, nor
even once she has had the vision; let all about her fall to pieces, so
she would have it that she may be wholly with This, so huge the happiness she has won to.

Such in this union is the soul's temper that even the act of intellect once so intimately loved she now dismisses; intellection is
movement and she has no wish to move; the object of her vision has
itself, she says, no intellection, even though it is by means of the
Intellectual-Principle that she has attained the vision, herself made
over into Intellectual-Principle and becoming that principle so as to
be able to take stand in that intellectual space. Entered there and
making herself over to that, she at first contemplates that realm, but
once she sees that higher still she leaves all else aside... In this state
of absorbed contemplation there is no longer question of holding an
object: the vision is continuous so that seeing and seen are one thing;
object and act of vision have become identical; of all that until then
filled the eye no memory remains.

Plotinus, *Ennead VI*

> *The vision of God,*
> *when he reveals himself to the soul,*
> *transports the soul to such a state of joy*
> *that we cannot imagine it.*

THE JOY OF LIFE ABUNDANT

I AM Life, I am All. Feel this truth vibrate within you until it becomes part of you. Truth can only be revealed from within. You can read about truth, you can be taught about it; but until you experience it within it does not become part of you and is therefore not reality. Once it has been revealed from within, it is there from everlasting to everlasting and nothing anyone can say or teach can alter it. Let all my truths be revealed from within.

Wait upon me in absolute stillness and you will behold the reality of life, life eternal, life more abundant. Life must be full, vibrant, glorious. I am all things to all people, therefore feel Me pulsating through your whole being, feel the joy and harmony welling up within you, pouring out of you, ever moving.

Be still, be very very still, and listen intently to all I have to say to you so you are ready and prepared at all times to do my will and obey My word without hesitation. My ways are not human ways, therefore expect the unexpected, be surprised at nothing. [...]

You are all mightily blessed. Take nothing for granted but give constant thanks for all My good and perfect gifts which are being poured down upon you all the time. Leave all in My hands, never try to manipulate anything or anyone. Let Me work My wonders in and through each individual. Simply be and let My divine love radiate in and through you.

Keep your consciousness raised and find that perfect state of stillness and do all from that; then behold My wonders and glories. Do all that unites and creates harmony and oneness and ignore all else. You are all my beloved children no matter who you are or where you are. Open your hearts and keep them open. See the very best in everyone and concentrate on that, drawing it forth and ignoring all that is negative.

Lift, lift, lift, and above all else love.

Eileen Caddy, *The Dawn of Change*

God is the truth and the joy in me;
in stillness I realize his truth
and the joy of life and love.

6 MYSTERY OF GOD

THE DIVINE MANIFESTATION

The full moon appeared in the night of hair,
and the black narcissus bedewed the rose.
A tender girl is she: the fair women were confounded by her,
and her radiance outshone the moon.
If she enters into the mind, that imagination wounds her:
how, then, can she be perceived by the eye?
She is a phantom of delight that melts away when we think of her:
she is too subtle for the range of vision.
Description sought to explain her, but she was transcendent,
and description became dumb.
Whenever it tries to qualify her,
it always retires baffled.
If one who seeks her will give rest to his beasts,
others will not give rest to the beast of reflection.
She is a joy that transports from the rank of humanity
every one who burns with love of her,
From jealousy that her clear essence should be mingled
with the filth that is in the tanks.
She excels the sun in splendour:
her form is not to be compared with any.
The heaven of light is under the sole of her foot:
her diadem is beyond the spheres.

Ibn Al-Arabi, *Tarjuman Al-Ashwaq*

*The divine Manifestation is as the light of the moon:
radiant and beautiful, delicate and elusive,
splendour and joy beyond description.*

THE BRILLIANT DARKNESS

TRINITY! Higher than any being,
  any divinity, any goodness!
Guide of Christians in the wisdom of heaven!
Lead us up beyond unknowing and light,
  up to the farthest, highest peak of mystic scripture
where the mysteries of God's Word
  lie simple, absolute and unchangeable
  in the brilliant darkness of a hidden silence.
Amid the deepest shadow
  they pour overwhelming light
  on what is most manifest.
Amid the wholly unsensed and unseen
  they completely fill our sightless minds
  with treasures beyond all beauty. [...]

What has actually to be said about the cause of everything is this.
Since it is the cause of all beings, we should posit and ascribe to it
all the affirmations we make in regard to beings, and, more appro-
priately, we should negate all these affirmations, since it surpasses
all being. Now we should not conclude that the negations are simply
the opposites of the affirmations, but rather that the cause of all is
considerably prior to this, beyond privations, beyond every denial,
beyond every assertion. [...]

The holiest and highest of the things perceived with the eye of the
body or the mind are but the rationale which presupposes all that lies
below the Transcendent One. Through them, however, his unimag-
inable presence is shown, walking the heights of those holy places
to which the mind at least can rise. But then he [Moses] breaks free
of them, away from what sees and is seen, and he plunges into the
truly mysterious darkness of unknowing. Here, renouncing all that
the mind may conceive, wrapped entirely in the intangible and the
invisible, he belongs completely to him who is beyond everything.
Here, being neither oneself nor someone else, one is supremely united by a completely unknowing inactivity of all knowledge, and
knows beyond the mind by knowing nothing. [...]

The cause of all is above all and is not inexistent, lifeless, speechless, mindless. It is not a material body, and hence has neither shape nor form, quality, quantity, or weight. It is not in any place and can neither be seen nor be touched. It is neither perceived nor is it perceptible. It suffers neither disorder nor disturbance and is overwhelmed by no earthly passion. It is not powerless and subject to the disturbances caused by sense perception. It endures no deprivation of light. It passes through no change, decay, division, loss, no ebb and flow, nothing of which the senses may be aware. None of all this can either be identified with it nor attributed to it.

Again, as we climb higher we say this. It is not soul or mind, nor does it possess imagination, conviction, speech, or understanding. Nor is it speech *per se*, understanding *per se*. It cannot be spoken of and it cannot be grasped by understanding. It is not number or order, greatness or smallness, equality or inequality, similarity or dissimilarity. It is not immovable, moving, or at rest. It has no power, it is not power, nor is it light. It does not live nor is it life. It is not a substance, nor is it eternity or time. It cannot be grasped by the understanding since it is neither knowledge nor truth. It is not kingship. It is not wisdom. It is neither one nor oneness, divinity nor goodness. Nor is it a spirit, in the sense in which we understand that term. It is not sonship or fatherhood and it is nothing known to us or to any other being. It falls neither within the predicate of non-being nor of being. Existing beings do not know it as it actually is and it does not know them as they are. There is no speaking of it, nor name nor knowledge of it. Darkness and light, error and truth – it is none of these. It is beyond assertion and denial. We make assertions and denials of what is next to it, but never of it, for it is both beyond every assertion, being the perfect and unique cause of all things, and, by virtue of its preeminently simple and absolute nature, free of every limitation, beyond every limitation; it is also beyond every denial.

Pseudo-Dionysius, *The Mystical Theology*

The Absolute Cause of all, the Transcendent,
is beyond our every assertion:
we come to it only by the unknowing
of faith and by love.

I AM SHIVA, ONLY SHIVA

I AM neither spirit, nor mind, nor the thinker. I am not the ego, nor a "self" composed of sense organs. I am neither air, nor light, nor earth, nor sky. I am Shiva, only Shiva, the eternal conscious bliss.

I am neither the breath of life, nor the five humours of man. I am not water, nor the aggregation of the constituent elements. I am not the five envelopes of the individual. I am not speech. I am neither hand, nor foot, nor generative organ. I am Shiva, only Shiva, the eternal conscious bliss.

I am neither love, nor hate, nor envy, nor attachment, nor pride, nor boastfulness. I am neither virtue, nor object of desire, nor passion, nor release. I am Shiva, only Shiva, the eternal conscious bliss.

I am neither merit, nor unmerit, nor happiness, nor suffering. I am not sacred hymns, nor a place of pilgrimage, nor the Vedas, nor the sacrifices. I am not the food itself, nor he who consumes food, nor that which is consumed. I am Shiva, only Shiva, the eternal conscious bliss.

In me there is no fear of death, nor are there distinctions of caste. I have no father, no mother, nor am I ever born. I have no parents, nor friends, nor master, nor disciple. I am Shiva, only Shiva, the eternal conscious bliss.

I do not doubt, nor do I believe. I penetrate all and in every respect. I am ever the same, neither bound, nor free. I am Shiva, only Shiva, the eternal conscious bliss.

Shankaracharya, *Nirvan Sthotra*

> *I am not anything that*
> *can be perceived, imagined or thought:*
> *yet I am everywhere, ever unchanging:*
> *I am Shiva, the eternal conscious bliss.*

THE FORMLESS FORM

WE LOOK but do not see:
  we call it the invisible.
We listen but do not hear:
  we call it the inaudible.
We grope but do not touch:
  we call it the intangible.
These three cannot be further examined
  and hence are bound together as one.

Rising up, it brings no light,
Coming down, it brings no darkness.
Infinite, it is nameless,
  and reverts to nothingness.
It is called the form of the formless,
  the image of the imageless;
It is the evanescent illusive.

Meet it, you cannot see its face.
Follow it, you cannot see its back.
Hold fast to the Way of old
  to master the things of the present;
To know what was in the beginning
  is called the heart of the Way.

Lao Tzu, *Tao Te Ching*, XIV

> *The Way is here and now:*
> *it cannot be seen, heard or touched:*
> *I follow it without knowing*
> *what it is, where it leads.*

THAT ALONE IS BRAHMAN

WHO sends the mind to wander afar? Who first drives life to start on its journey? Who impels us to utter these words? Who is the Spirit behind the eye and the ear?

It is the ear of the ear, the eye of the eye, and the Word of words, the mind of mind, and the life of life. Those who follow wisdom pass beyond and, on leaving this world, become immortal.

There the eye goes not, nor word, nor mind. We know not, we cannot understand, how he can be explained: He is above the known and he is above the unknown. Thus have we heard from the ancient sages who explained this truth to us.

What cannot be spoken with words, but that whereby words are spoken: Know that alone to be Brahman, the Spirit; and not what people here adore.

What cannot be thought with the mind, but that whereby the mind can think: Know that alone to be Brahman, the Spirit; and not what people here adore.

What cannot be seen with the eye, but that whereby the eye can see: Know that alone to be Brahman, the Spirit; and not what people here adore.

What cannot be heard with the ear, but that whereby the ear can hear: Know that alone to be Brahman, the Spirit; and not what people here adore.

What cannot be indrawn with breath, but that whereby breath is indrawn: Know that alone to be Brahman, the Spirit; and not what people here adore.

If you think "I know well," little truth you know. You only perceive that appearance of Brahman that lies in the senses and is in you. [...]

I do not imagine "I know him well," and yet I cannot say "I know him not." Who of us knows this, knows him; and not who says "I know him not."

He comes to the thought of those who know him beyond thought, not to those who imagine that he can be attained by thought. He is unknown to the learned and known to the simple.

He is known in the ecstasy of an awakening which opens the door of life eternal. By the Self we obtain power, and by vision we obtain eternity.

For a man who has known him, the light of truth shines; for one who has not known, there is darkness. The wise who have seen him in every being, on leaving this life, attain life immortal.

Kena Upanishad, 1-2

> *That which my soul seeks*
> *is the very principle of life and activity;*
> *it is not here below,*
> *but neither is it unknown to my soul.*

THE INCOMPREHENSIBLE

HIS judgements are inscrutable, his ways unsearchable, his peace surpasses all understanding, his gift is indescribable, what God has prepared for those who love him has not entered into the heart of man, his greatness has no bound, his understanding is infinite. Are all these incomprehensible while only God himself can be comprehended? What excessive madness would it be to say that?

Stop the heretic; do not let him get away. Tell me. What does Paul say? "Our knowledge is imperfect" (*1 Corinthians*, 13). The heretic answers that Paul is not talking about God's essence but about his governance of the universe. Very good then. If he is talking about the governance of the universe, our victory is all the more complete. For if his governance of the universe is incomprehensible, then all the more so is God himself beyond our powers of comprehension. But so that you may know that Paul is not talking here about God's governance of the universe but about God himself, listen to what follows.

After Paul said: "Our knowledge is imperfect and our prophesying is imperfect," he went on to say: "My knowledge is imperfect now; then I shall know even as I was known." By whom, then, was he known? Was it by God or by the governance of the universe? Clearly, it was by God. Therefore, he is saying that his present knowledge of God is imperfect and in part. Paul did not say "imperfect" because he knows one part of God's essence and does not know another part – for God is simple and has no parts.

He said this because on the one hand he knows that God exists, whereas, on the other, he does not know what God is in his essence. He knows that God is wise but he does not know how great his wisdom is. He knows that God is great but he does not know how or what his greatness is. He also knows that God is everywhere present but he does not know how this is so. He knows that God provides for all things and that he preserves and governs them to perfection. But he does not know the way in which God does all these things. Therefore, he said: "Our knowledge is imperfect and our prophesying is imperfect." [...]

Let us call upon him, then, as the ineffable God who is beyond our intelligence, invisible, incomprehensible, who transcends the power of mortal words. Let us call on him as the God who is inscrutable to the angels, unseen by the Seraphim, inconceivable to the Cherubim, invisible to the Principalities, to the Powers, and to the Virtues, in fact to all creatures without qualification, because he is known only by the Son and the Spirit.

John Chrysostom,
On the Incomprehensible Nature of God, I & III

God is: how he is, how he acts,
I can know only in part:
may I accept that he is incomprehensible,
save as he reveals himself.

THE MYSTERY OF THE TAO

WHAT is this thing called the Way? There is the Way of Heaven and the way of man. To rest in inaction and command respect – this is the Way of Heaven. To engage in action and become entangled in it – this is the way of man. The ruler is the Way of Heaven; his subjects are the way of men. The Way of Heaven and the way of man are far apart. This is something to consider carefully!

*   *   *

The Great Way is not named; Great Discriminations are not spoken; Great Benevolence is not benevolent; Great Modesty is not humble; Great Daring does not attack. If the Way is made clear, it is not the Way. If discriminations are put into words, they do not suffice. If benevolence has a constant object, it cannot be universal. If modesty is fastidious, it cannot be trusted. If daring attacks, it cannot be complete. These five are all round, but they tend toward the square.

Therefore understanding that rests in what it does not understand is the finest. Who can understand discriminations that are not spoken, the Way that is not a way? If he can understand this, he may be called the Reservoir of Heaven. Pour into it and it is never full, dip from it and it never runs dry, and yet it does not know where the supply comes from.

*   *   *

The Way has its reality and its signs but is without action or form. You can hand it down but you cannot receive it; you can get it but you cannot see it. It is its own source, its own root. Before heaven and earth existed it was there, firm from ancient times. It gave spirituality to the spirits and to God; it gave birth to heaven and to earth. It exists beyond the highest point, and yet you cannot call it lofty; it exists beneath the limit of the six directions, and yet you cannot call it deep. It was born before heaven and earth, and yet you cannot say it has been there for long; it is earlier than the earliest time, and yet you cannot call it old.

*   *   *

I will tell you about the Perfect Way. The essence of the Perfect Way is deep and darkly shrouded; the extreme of the Perfect Way is mysterious and hushed in silence. Let there be no seeing, no hearing; enfold the spirit in quietude and the body will right itself. Be still, be pure, do not labour your body, do not churn up your essence, and then you can live a long life. When the eye does not see, the ear does not hear, and the mind does not know, then your spirit will protect the body, and the body will enjoy long life. Be cautious of what is within you; block off what is outside you, for much knowledge will do you harm. Then I will lead you up above the Great Brilliance, to the source of the Perfect Yang; I will guide you through the dark and mysterious gate, to the source of the Perfect Yin.

* * *

The Way is without beginning or end, but things have their life and death – you cannot rely upon their fulfilment. One moment empty, the next moment full – you cannot depend upon their form. The years cannot be held off; time cannot be stopped. Decay, growth, fullness and emptiness end and then begin again. It is thus that we must describe the plan of the Great Meaning and discuss the principles of the ten thousand things. The life of things is a gallop, a headlong dash – with every movement they alter, with every moment they shift. What should you do and what should you not do? Everything will change of itself, that is certain!

The Book of Chuang Tzu

The Tao of heaven is immutable and eternal;
mysterious and silent, the origin of all things,
beyond all which is born, lives and dies.

THE ONE NATURE

THE DUST [of ignorance] has been since of old
    accumulating on the mirror never polished,
Now is the time once for all to see
    the clearing positively done.

                    *   *   *

Ignorance in reality is the Buddha-nature,
This empty visionary body
    is no less than the Dharma-body.
When one knows what the Dharma-body is,
    there is not an object [to be known as such],
The source of all things, as far as its self-nature goes,
    is the Buddha in his absolute aspect.

                    *   *   *

Only let us take hold of the root
    and not worry about the branches;
It is like a crystal basin reflecting the moon,
And I know now what this *mani*-gem is,
Whereby not only oneself is benefited
    but others, inexhaustibly;
The moon is serenely reflected on the stream,
    the breeze passes softly through the pines,
Perfect silence reigning unruffled -
    what is it for?

                    *   *   *

The Mind like a mirror is brightly illuminating
    and knows no obstructions,
It penetrates the vast universe
    to its minutest crevices;
All its contents, multitudinous in form,
    are reflected in the Mind,
Which, shining like a perfect gem,
    has no surface, nor the inside.

                    *   *   *

One nature, perfect and pervading,
    circulates in all natures;
One Reality, all comprehensive,

contains within itself all realities;
One moon is reflected
   wherever there is a sheet of water,
And all the moons in all the waters
   are embraced within the one moon.
The Dharma-body of all the Buddhas
   enters into my own being,
And my own being is found in union with theirs.

              *   *   *

[This inner Light] is beyond both praise and abuse,
Like unto space it knows no boundaries;
Yet it is right here with us
   ever retaining its serenity and fullness.
It is only when you seek it that you lose it.
You cannot take hold of it,
   nor can you get rid of it;
While you can do neither,
   it goes on its own way.
You remain silent and it speaks;
   you speak and it is silent.
The great gate of heaven is wide open
   with no obstructions whatever before it.

              *   *   *

The mind functions through sense-organs, and
   thereby an objective world is comprehended -
This dualism marks darkly on the mirror;
When the dirt is wiped off,
   the light shines out;
So when both the mind and the objective world are forgotten,
   the Essence asserts its truth.

     Yung-chia Ta-shih (Yoka Daishi), *Song of Enlightenment*

> *All that is,*
> *is but one Reality:*
> *my real nature is that*
> *of all the Buddhas.*

THE MYSTERY SUPREME

BECAUSE you are never envious of me, O Arjuna, I shall give you this most secret wisdom, knowing which you will be relieved from the miseries of material existence. This knowledge is the king of education, the most secret of all secrets. It is the purest knowledge, and because it gives direct perception of the self by realization, it is the perfection of religion. It is everlasting and joyfully performed. Those who are not faithful on the path of devotional service, O killer of the enemies, cannot achieve me. Therefore, they come back to birth and death in this material world.

In my unmanifested form I pervade all this creation. All things are resting in me, but I am not in them. Again, everything that is created does not rest on me. Behold my mystic opulence! Although I am the maintainer of all living entities and although I am everywhere, still my self is the very source of creation. As in the great sky the wind is blowing everywhere, so all the cosmic manifestation is situated in me. O son of Kunti, at the end of the millennium every material manifestation enters unto my nature, and at the beginning of another millennium, by my potency, I again create. The whole cosmic order is under me. By my will it is manifested again and again, and by my will it is annihilated at the end. O Dhananjaya, all this work cannot bind me. I am ever detached, seated as though neutral. [...]

The foolish mock at me, at my descending like a human being. They do not know my transcendental nature and my supreme dominion over all that be. Those who are thus bewildered are attracted by demoniac and atheistic views. In that deluded condition, their hopes for liberation, their fruitive activities and their culture of knowledge are all defeated. O son of Partha, those who are not deluded, the great souls, are under the protection of the divine nature. They are fully engaged in devotional service because they know me as the Supreme Personality of Godhead, original and inexhaustible. They are always chanting my glories. Endeavouring with great determination, offering homage to me, they worship me with devotion. Others, who are engaged in the cultivation of knowledge, worship the Supreme Lord as the one without a second, as diverse in many and in the universal form. But it is I who am the ritual, I the sacrifice, the offering to the ancestors, the healing herb, the transcendental chant; I am the butter and the fire and the offering. I am the father, mother, maintainer and grandfather of all this universe. I am what is to be known, I am purity, and I am the syllable OM. I am the Rig, Sama and Yajur [Vedas]. I am the goal, the upholder, the master, the witness, the home, the shelter and the most dear friend. I am the creation and the annihilation, the basis of everything, the resting place and the eternal seed. O Arjuna, I control heat, the rain and the drought. I am immortality, and I am death personified. Both being and nonbeing are in me. [...]

Those who devote themselves steadfastly to me, meditating on my transcendental form, receive all bounties and securities from me. [...] If one offers me with love and devotion a leaf, a flower, fruit, or water, I will accept it. O son of Kunti, all that you do, all that you eat, all that you offer and give away, as well as all austerities that you may perform, should be done as an offering unto me. Thus you will be free of all reactions to good and evil deeds, and by this principle of renunciation you will be liberated and come to me. I envy no one, nor am I partial to anyone. I am equal to all. But whoever renders service unto me in devotion is a friend, is in me, and I am a friend to him. [...] O son of Kunti, declare it boldly that my devotee will never perish.

O son of Partha, anyone who takes shelter in me – even a woman, a merchant or one who is born in a low family – can approach the supreme destination. How much greater are the *brahmanas*, the righteous, the devotees and saintly kings who in this temporary, miserable world engage in devotional service to the Lord. Engage your mind always in thinking of me, become my devotee, engage your body in my service, and surrender unto me. Completely absorbed in me, surely you will come to me.

Bhagavad Gita, 9

---

*I am the origin and the sustainer
of all beings in this universe;
those who know this and love me
come to me and achieve eternal peace.*

DESIRE TO BE NOTHING

TO reach satisfaction in all
  desire satisfaction in nothing.
To come to possess all
  desire the possession of nothing.
To arrive at being all
  desire to be nothing.
To come to the knowledge of all
  desire the knowledge of nothing.

To come to enjoy what you have not
  you must go by a way in which you enjoy not.
To come to the knowledge you have not
  you must go by a way in which you know not.
To come to the possession you have not
  you must go by a way in which you possess not.
To come to be what you are not
  you must go by a way in which you are not.

When you delay in something
  you cease to rush toward the all.
For to go from the all to the all
  you must deny yourself of all in all.
And when you come to the possession of the all
  you must possess it without wanting anything.
Because if you desire to have something in all
  your treasure in God is not purely your all.

In this nakedness the spirit finds its quietude and rest. For in coveting nothing, nothing tires it and nothing oppresses it, because it is in the centre of its humility.

John of the Cross, *The Ascent of Mount Carmel*, I, 13

I see nothing, I feel nothing,
I know nothing, I am nothing:
naked I come before you, my God, my All.

NOT KNOWING WHY

NOT knowing why, not knowing why -
This is my support;
Not knowing why -
This is the *"Namu-amida-butsu."*

* * *

As I pronounce *"Namu-amida-butsu"*
I feel my thoughts and hindrances are like the spring snows:
They thaw away as soon as they fall on the ground.

* * *

Saichi has nothing – which is joy.
Outside this there's nothing.
Both good and evil – all's taken away,
Nothing's left.
To have nothing – this is the release, this is the peace.
All's taken away by the *"Namu-amida-butsu,"*
This is truly the peace. *"Namu-amida-butsu!"*

* * *

Nothing is left to Saichi,
Except a joyful heart, nothing is left to him;
Neither good nor bad has he, all is taken away from him;
Nothing is left to him!
To have nothing – how completely satisfying!
Everything has been carried away by the *"Namu-amida-butsu."*
He is thoroughly at home with himself:
This is indeed the *"Namu-amida-butsu"*!

* * *

Everything of mine has been carried away by thee,
And thou hast given me the *Nembutsu* -
"Namu-amida-butsu."

Saichi, *Journals*

To accept not knowing why:
to have nothing, yet to have everything:
the place of peace within.

THE MASTER-WEAVER OF MAGIC

HOW, O brother, is existence contained in non-existence? How is the opposite concealed in opposite? *He brings forth the living from the dead:* know that the hope of his worshippers is non-existence. [...]

Non-existence is God's factory from which he continually produces gifts. God is the originator, and an originator is he who produces a branch without root or support. God has caused the non-existent to appear existent and magnificent; he has caused the existent to appear in the form of non-existence. He has concealed the sea and made the foam visible; he has concealed the wind and displayed to you the dust. The dust is whirling in the air, high as a minaret: how should the dust rise aloft of itself?

You see the dust on high, O infirm of sight: the wind you see not, except through knowledge given by induction. You see the foam moving in every direction: without the sea the foam has no turning-place. You see the foam by sense-perception and the sea by induction: thought is hidden, speech manifest.

We deemed negation to be affirmation: we had an eye that saw only the non-existent. The eye that came into being in a state of slumber (the present life), how should it be able to see anything but fantasy and non-existence? Necessarily we were bewildered by error, since reality was hidden and fantasy visible. We wonder why God set up this non-existence in full view and why he caused that reality to be hidden from sight.

Praise to you, O Master-weaver of magic, who has made the dregs to seem pure wine to them that turn away from the truth. Magicians quickly measure moonbeams in the presence of the merchant and receive gold as profit. When by artful tricks of this sort they take money, the money is gone from the purchaser's hand, but there is no linen to be seen. This world is a sorcerer, and we are the merchants who buy from it the measured moonbeams. Magician-like, it hastily measures out by the ell five hundred ells of linen from the light of the moonbeams, yet, when it takes your money, which is your life, O slave, the money is gone, there is no linen, and your purse is empty. You must recite *Say, I take refuge* (*Koran*, 43, 1), crying, "O you who are one, come, save me from the witches and from their knots. These sorceresses are blowing on the knots: help,

O you whose help is sought against the world's victory and triumph."

Jalal od-Din Rumi, *Mathnawi*, V

Behind the veil of illusions
of this visible world,
God is the sole existence,
the only reality.

THE SECRET SAYINGS OF JESUS

THESE are the secret sayings which the living Jesus spoke, and which Didymos Judas Thomas wrote down.

And he said, "Whoever finds the interpretation of these sayings will not experience death."

Jesus said: "Let him who seeks continue seeking until he finds. When he finds, he will become troubled. When he becomes troubled, he will be astonished, and he will rule over the all."

Jesus said, "If those who lead you say to you, 'See, the kingdom is in the sky,' then the birds of the sky will precede you. If they say to you, 'It is in the sea,' then the fish will precede you. Rather, the kingdom is inside of you, and it is outside of you. When you come to know yourselves, then you will become known, and you will realize that it is you who are the sons of the living father. But if you do not know yourselves, you dwell in poverty and it is you who are the poverty."

Jesus said, "Recognize what is in your sight, and that which is hidden from you will become plain to you. For there is nothing hidden which will not become manifest."

Jesus said: "This heaven will pass away, and the one above it will pass away. The dead are not alive, and the living will not die. In the days when you consumed what is dead, you made it what is alive. When you come to dwell in the light, what will you do? On the day when you were one you became two. But when you become two, what will you do?"

Jesus said: "Compare me to someone and tell me whom I am like." Simon Peter said to him, "You are like a righteous angel." Matthew said to him, "You are like a wise philosopher." Thomas said to him, "Master, my mouth is wholly incapable of saying whom you are like." Jesus said, "I am not your master. Because you have drunk, you have become intoxicated from the bubbling spring which I have measured out."

Jesus said: "I shall give you what no eye has seen and what no ear has heard and what no hand had touched and what has never occurred to the human mind."

Jesus said: "Blessed is he who came into being before he came into being. If you become my disciples and listen to my words, these stones will minister to you. For there are five trees for you in Paradise which will remain undisturbed summer and winter and whose leaves do not fall. Whoever becomes acquainted with them will not experience death."

Jesus said: "If one who knows the all still feels a personal deficiency, he is completely deficient."

Jesus said: "That which you have will save you if you bring it forth from yourselves. That which you do not have within you will kill you if you do not have it within you."

Jesus said, "It is I who am the light which is above them all. It is I who am the all. From me did the all come forth, and unto me did the all extend. Split a piece of wood, and I am there. Lift up the stone, and you will find me there."

Jesus said, "He who is near me is near the fire, and he who is far from me is far from the kingdom."

Jesus said, "The kingdom of the Father is like a certain woman who was carrying a jar full of meal. While she was walking on the road, still some distance from home, the handle of the jar broke and the meal emptied out behind her on the road. She did not realize it; she had noticed no accident. When she reached her house, she set the jar down and found it empty."

His disciples said to him, "When will the kingdom come?" Jesus said, "It will not come by waiting for it. Rather, the kingdom of the Father is spread out upon the earth, and men do not see it."

The Gospel of Thomas

The greatest mystery of life eternal:
the search for the kingdom of God
begins and ends with oneself.

THE MYSTERY OF THE ABSOLUTE

BRAHMAN is above and beyond *vidya* (the relative knowledge which leads towards God) as well as *avidya* (the world which keeps all beings away from the knowledge of God). Knowledge leading towards God is the last and topmost step of the stairs leading to the roof. The Absolute is the roof. The phenomenal world is made of that which leads towards God and that which does not. Thus God the Absolute is above and beyond the phenomenal world. The Absolute is unattached to good or evil. It is like the light of a lamp. You may read the Holy Scriptures with its help. It is equally open to you to forge another man's signature in the same light.

The Absolute is being not conditioned by anything – time, space or causation. How can one give expression to it by any word of mouth? The Absolute again is like the unfathomable ocean. Nothing can be predicated of it – the being beyond all bounds of relativity, of all existence. The last feeble attempt to describe this being, the attempt made in the Vedas, is to call him by the name of Bliss Everlasting.

The Great mystery defies all attempts at explanation. The Absolute and Unconditioned cannot be stated in terms of the relative, the conditioned; the Infinite cannot be expressed in terms of the finite.

He who has true knowledge ceases to have anything to do with talk or controversy. God the Absolute is the one Substance to be realized – not described or known. The sign of true knowledge or realization is cessation of doubt and therefore of all philosophical discussion.

The Higher Self (*atman*) alone knows the Higher Self. He, Knowledge Absolute, is capable of being realized by himself, the Knowledge Absolute alone. The differentiated soul, so long as it continues to be differentiated and walks on the lower plane, cannot as such realize God the Absolute. The Undifferentiated alone realizes the Undifferentiated. This is the true meaning of the expression "God is unknown and unknowable".

The Absolute is the only reality; the universe is unreal, that is, when looked at from the point of view of the Absolute. To the Absolute or the Undifferentiated the universe and man and other creatures are unreal, for the only reality is the Absolute. When *maya* is realized as unreal the differentiated ego has been completely shaken off or effaced, so to speak. There is no trace of the ego left behind; it is perfect *samadhi*.

It is absurd to say "the world is unreal" so long as we remain convinced that we ourselves are real! A person who has not realized the Absolute cannot realize that the world is unreal. On the other hand, a saint returning from samadhi to a lower spiritual plane gets back by my Mother's will, his differentiated, attenuated, though purified, ego.

The Gospel of Sri Ramakrishna

The Absolute and Unconditioned alone is real;
unknowable by human facilities,
it can be experienced, but never fully grasped.

THE EMISSARY OF THE POWER

I WAS sent forth from the Power,
  and I have come to those who reflect upon me,
  and I have been found among those who seek after me.
Look upon me, you who reflect upon me,
  and you hearers, hear me.
You who are waiting for me, take me to yourselves.
And do not banish me from your sight.
And do not make your voice hate me, nor your hearing.
Do not be ignorant of me anywhere or at any time.
Be on your guard!
Do not be ignorant of me.

For I am the first and the last.
I am the honoured one and the scorned one.
I am the whore and the holy one.
I am the wife and the virgin.
I am the mother and the daughter.
I am the members of my mother.
I am the barren one and many are her sons.
I am she whose wedding is great,
  and I have not taken a husband.
I am the midwife and she who does not bear.
I am the solace of my labour pains.
I am the bride and the bridegroom,
  and it is my husband who begot me.
I am the mother of my father, and the sister
  of my husband, and he is my offspring.
I am the slave of him who prepared me.
I am the ruler of my offspring.
But he is the one who begot me
  before the time on a birthday.
And he is my offspring in due time,
  and my power is from him.
I am the staff of his power in his youth,
  and he is the rod of my old age.
  And whatever he wills happens to me.

I am the silence that is incomprehensible
and the idea whose remembrance is frequent.
I am the voice whose sound is manifold
and the word whose appearance is multiple.
I am the utterance of my name.

Why, you who hate me, do you love me
and hate those who love me?
You who deny me, confess me,
and you who confess me, deny me.
You who tell the truth about me, lie about me,
and you who have lied about me, tell the truth about me.
You who know me, be ignorant of me,
and those who have not known me, let them know me. [...]

For what is inside of you is what is outside of you,
and the one who fashions you on the outside
is the one who shaped the inside of you.
And what you see outside of you,
you see inside of you; it is visible and is your garment.

Hear me, you hearers,
and learn of my words, you who know me.
I am the hearing that is attainable to everything;
I am the speech that cannot be grasped.
I am the name of the sound
and the sound of the name.

The Thunder: Perfect Mind
(Nag Hammadi Library)

We all originate from the same eternal Power;
it is she who fashioned both
our external appearance and our inner being;
after this terrestrial passage,
we return to her.

THE GATELESS GATE

The great Way, there is no gate,
There are a thousand different roads.
If one passes through the barrier once,
He will walk independently in the universe.

JOSHU'S DOG: A monk asked Joshu in all earnestness, "Has a dog Buddha nature or not?" Joshu said, "*Mu!*" [nothing, non-being]
Dog! Buddha nature!
The perfect manifestation, the absolute command;
A little "has" or "has not",
And body is lost! Life is lost!

BUDDHA'S FLOWER: Once in ancient times, when the World-Honoured One was at Vulture Peak to give a sermon, he held up a flower and showed it to the assemblage. At this they all remained silent. Only the venerable Kashyapa broke into a smile. The World-Honoured One said: "I have the eye treasury of the true Dharma, the marvellous mind of nirvana, the true form of no-form, the subtle gate of the Dharma. It does not depend on letters, being specially transmitted outside all teachings. Now I entrust Mahakashyapa with this."
Handling a flower,
The tail of the snake manifested itself.
Kashyapa breaks into a smile,
Nobody on earth or in heaven knows what to do.

WASH YOUR BOWLS: A monk asked Joshu in all earnestness: "I have just entered this monastery. I beg you, Master, please give me instructions." Joshu asked, "Have you eaten your rice gruel yet?" The monk answered, "Yes, I have." Joshu said: "Then wash your bowls."
Just because it is so clear
It takes us longer to realize it.
If you quickly acknowledge that the candlelight is fire,
You will find that the rice has long been cooked.

THE WIND AND THE FLAG: The wind was flapping a temple flag, and two monks were having an argument about it. One said, "The flag is moving." The other said, "The wind is moving." They argued back and forth but could not reach the truth. The sixth patriarch said, "It is not the wind that moves. It is not the flag that moves. It is your mind that moves."

The wind moves, the flag moves, the mind moves;
All have missed it.
They only know how to open their mouths,
And do not know that their words have failed.

MIND AND BUDDHA: Taibai asked Baso in all earnestness, "What is Buddha?" Baso answered, "The very mind is Buddha."

The blue sky, the bright day,
It is most detestable to hunt around;
If, furthermore, you ask, "What is Buddha?"
It is like shouting your innocence while holding the loot.

NO MIND, NO BUDDHA: A monk asked Baso in all earnestness, "What is Buddha?" Baso replied, "No mind, no Buddha."

If you meet a swordsman, you may present a sword;
You should not offer a poem unless you meet a poet.
When you speak to others, say only three-quarters of it;
You should never give the remaining part.

KNOWING IS NOT THE WAY: Nansen said, "Mind is not the Buddha; knowing is not the Way."

When the sky clears, the sun appears,
When the rain falls, the earth gets wet.
With all his heart, he has preached everything,
But I fear nobody can believe it.

Mumon Ekai, *Mumonkan* (Wumen Huikai, *Wumen Kuan*)

> *The sun rises, the candle burns,*
> *The mystery dawns in the morning dew.*
> *When mind and Buddha are the same,*
> *We see with our eyes, not our hands.*

7 SILENCE OF GOD

STANZAS OF THE SOUL

ONE dark night,
Fired with love's urgent longings
- Ah, the sheer grace! -
I went out unseen,
My house being now all stilled.

In darkness, and secure,
By the secret ladder, disguised,
- Ah, the sheer grace! -
In darkness and concealment,
My house being now all stilled.

On that glad night,
In secret, for no one saw me,
Nor did I look at anything,
With no other light or guide
Than the one that burned in my heart.

This guided me
More surely than the light of noon
To where he was waiting for me
- Him I knew so well -
There in a place where no one else appeared.

O guiding night!
O night more lovely than the dawn!
O night that has united
The Lover with his beloved,
Transforming the beloved in her Lover.

Upon my flowering breast
Which I kept wholly for him alone,
There he lay sleeping,
And I caressing him
There in a breeze from the fanning cedars.

When the breeze blew from the turret,
As I parted his hair,
It wounded my neck
With its gentle hand,
Suspending all my senses.

I abandoned and forgot myself,
Laying my face on my Beloved;
All things ceased; I went out from myself,
Leaving my cares
Forgotten among the lilies.

John of the Cross, *The Dark Night*, Prologue

> *God's love alone guides me through*
> *the dark night of my soul;*
> *it leads me into his divine light.*

"ONE DARK NIGHT"

THIS dark night is an inflow of God into the soul, which purges it of its habitual ignorances and imperfections, natural and spiritual, and which the contemplatives call infused contemplation or mystical theology. Through this contemplation, God teaches the soul secretly and instructs it in the perfection of love without its doing anything or understanding how this happens.

Insofar as infused contemplation is loving wisdom of God, it produces two principal effects in the soul; by both purging and illumining, this contemplation prepares the soul for the union with God through love. Hence the same loving wisdom that purges and illumines the blessed spirits purges and illumines the soul here on earth.

Yet a doubt arises: Why, if it is a divine light (for it illumines and purges them of their ignorance), does the soul call it a dark night? In answer to this, there are two reasons this divine wisdom is not only night and darkness for the soul, but also affliction and torment. First, because of the height of the divine wisdom that exceeds the abilities of the soul; and on this account the wisdom is dark for the soul. Second, because of the soul's baseness and impurity; and on this account the wisdom is painful, afflictive, and also dark for the soul.

To prove the first reason, we must presuppose a certain principle of the Philosopher [Aristotle]: that the clearer and more obvious divine things are in themselves, the darker and more hidden they are to the soul naturally. The brighter the light, the more the owl is blinded; and the more one looks at the brilliant sun, the more the sun darkens the faculty of sight, deprives and overwhelms it in its weakness.

Hence when the divine light of contemplation strikes a soul not yet entirely illumined, it causes spiritual darkness, for it not only surpasses the act of natural understanding but it also deprives the soul of this act and darkens it. This is why St. Dionysius and other mystical theologians call this infused contemplation a "ray of darkness" – that is, for the soul not yet illumined and purged. For this great supernatural light overwhelms the intellect and deprives it of its natural vigour. [...]

It is also evident that this dark contemplation is painful to the soul in these beginnings. Since this divine infused contemplation has many extremely good properties, and the still unpurged soul that receives it has many extreme miseries, and because two contraries cannot coexist in one subject, the soul must necessarily undergo affliction and suffering. Because of the purgation of its imperfections caused by this contemplation, the soul becomes a battlefield in which these two contraries combat one another. We shall prove this by induction in the following way.

In regard to the first cause of one's affliction: because the light and wisdom of this contemplation is very bright and pure, and the soul in which it shines is dark and impure, a person will be deeply afflicted on receiving it. When eyes are sickly, impure, and weak, they suffer pain if a bright light shines on them. The soul, because of its impurity, suffers immensely at the time this divine light truly assails it. When this pure light strikes in order to expel all impurity, persons feel so unclean and wretched that it seems God is against them and that they are against God. [...]

Persons suffer affliction in the second manner because of their natural, moral and spiritual weakness. Since this divine contemplation assails them somewhat forcibly in order to subdue and strengthen their souls, they suffer so much in their weakness that they almost die, particularly at times when the light is more powerful. Both the sense and the spirit, as though under an immense and dark load, undergo such agony and pain that the soul would consider death a relief [...]

How amazing and pitiful it is that the soul be so utterly weak and impure that the hand of God, though light and gentle, should feel so heavy and contrary. For the hand of God does not press down or weigh on the soul, but only touches it; and this mercifully, for God's aim is to grant it favours and not to chastise it.

John of the Cross, *The Dark Night*, II

As the brightness of the sun at midday,
the brilliance of divine light blinds the soul:
the dark night, in which God reveals himself.

HE WILL FLEE

OH seize the hem of his favour,
   for suddenly he will flee!
But do not draw him like arrows,
   for from the bow he will flee.

Look – all the shapes he assumes, and
   what kind of tricks he plays!
In form he may well be present,
   but from the soul he will flee.

You seek him high in his heaven -
   he shines like the moon in a lake,
But if you enter the water,
   up to the sky he will flee.

You seek him in where-no-place is -
   then he gives signs of his place:
But if you seek him in places,
   to where-no-place he will flee.

As arrows fly from the bowstring
   and like the bird of your thought...
You know for sure; from the doubting
   the Absolute One will flee.

"I'll flee from this and from that, see -
   but not out of weariness:
I fear that my beauty, so lovely,
   from this and from that may well flee.

For like the wind I am flighty,
   I love the rose, like the breeze,
But out of fear of the autumn,
   you see, the rose too will flee!"

His name will flee when it sees you
   intent on pronouncing it.
So that you cannot tell others:
   "Look here, such a person will flee!"

He'll flee from you if you try then
   to sketch his picture and form -
The picture flees from the tablet,
   the sign from the heart will flee!

Jalal od-Din Rumi, *Diwan-i-Shams-i-Tabriz*

---

*The One always flees
from our attempts to seize him
with perceptions and concepts:
we have only fleeting glimpses of him.*

THE DHARMA OF THE ABSOLUTE STATE

VIMALAKIRTI said to the bodhisattvas present: "Virtuous Ones, each of you please say something about the non-dual dharma as you understand it."

In the assembly a bodhisattva called "Comfort in the Dharma" said: "Virtuous Ones, birth and death are a duality but nothing is created and nothing is destroyed. Realization of this patient endurance leading to the uncreate is initiation into the non-dual dharma."

The bodhisattva called "Guardian of the Three Virtues" said: "Subject and object are a duality for where there is ego there is also its object, but since fundamentally there is no ego, its object does not arise; this is initiation into the non-dual dharma." [...]

The bodhisattva "Highest Virtue" said: "Impurity and purity are a duality. When the underlying nature of impurity is clearly perceived, even purity ceases to arise. Hence this cessation (of the idea of purity) is initiation into the non-dual dharma."

The bodhisattva "Achiever of Samadhi by Looking at the Star" said: "External disturbance and inner thinking are a duality; when disturbance subsides, thinking comes to an end and the absence of thought leads to non-discriminating; reaching this state is initiation into the non-dual dharma." [...]

The bodhisattva "Pure Interpretation" said: "Activity and non-activity are a duality, but if the mind is kept from all mental conditions it will be void like space and pure and clean wisdom will be free from all obstructions. This is initiation into the non-dual dharma." [...]

The Bodhisattva Priyadarsana said: "Form and voidness are a duality, but form is identical with voidness, which does not mean that form wipes out voidness, for the underlying nature of form is void itself. So are the other four aggregates, reception, conception, discrimination and consciousness. Consciousness and voidness are a duality yet consciousness is identical with voidness, which does not mean that consciousness wipes out voidness for the underlying nature of voidness is void of itself. A thorough understanding of this is initiation into the non-dual dharma." [...]

The bodhisattva "Joy in Reality" said: "Reality and unreality are a duality, but he who realizes reality does not even perceive it, still less unreality. Why? Because reality is invisible to the ordinary eyes and appears only to the eye of wisdom. Thus realization of the eye of wisdom, which is neither observant nor unobservant, is initiation into the non-dual dharma."

After the bodhisattvas had spoken, they asked Manjusri for his opinion on the non-dual dharma. Manjusri said: "In my opinion, when all things are no longer within the province of either word or speech, and of either indication or knowledge, and are beyond questions and answers, this is initiation into the non-dual dharma."

Thereat, Manjusri asked Vimalakirti: "All of us have spoken; please tell us what is the bodhisattva's initiation into the non-dual dharma."

Vimalakirti kept silent without saying a word.

At that, Manjusri exclaimed: "Excellent, excellent; can there be true initiation into the non-dual dharma until words and speech are no longer written or spoken?"

Vimalakirti Nirdesa Sutra, IX

Silence of the body, silence of the spirit:
this is the way to the realization
of non-duality and its very essence.

THE ABANDONED OF GOD

MY God, my God, why have you forsaken me?
Why are you so far from helping me,
     from the words of my groaning?
O my God, I cry by day, but you do not answer,
     and by night, but find no rest.

Yet you are holy, enthroned on the praises of Israel.
In you our ancestors trusted;
     they trusted, and you delivered them.
To you they cried, and were saved;
     in you they trusted, and were not put to shame.

But I am a worm, and not human;
     scorned by others, and despised by the people.
All who see me mock at me;
     they make mouths at me, they shake their heads;
"Commit your cause to the Lord; let him deliver -
     let him rescue the one in whom he delights!"

Yet it was you who took me from the womb;
     you kept me safe on my mother's breast.
On you I was cast from my birth,
     and since my mother bore me
     you have been my God.
Do not be far from me, for trouble is near
     and there is no one to help.

Many bulls encircle me,
     strong bulls of Bashan surround me;
They open wide their mouths at me,
     like a ravening and roaring lion.

I am poured out like water,
     and all my bones are out of joint;
My heart is like wax;
     it is melted within my breast;

My mouth is dried up like a potsherd,
   and my tongue sticks to my jaws;
   you lay me in the dust of death.

For dogs are all around me;
   a company of evildoers encircles me.

My hands and feet have shrivelled;
   I can count all my bones.
They stare and gloat over me;
   they divide my clothes among themselves;
   and for my clothing they cast lots.

But you, O Lord, do not be far away!
   O my help, come quickly to my aid!
Deliver my soul from the sword,
   my life from the power of the dog!
Save me from the mouth of the lion!

From the horns of the wild oxen
   you have rescued me.
I will tell of your name to my brothers and sisters;
   in the midst of the congregation I will praise you:
You who fear the Lord, praise him!
All you offspring of Jacob, glorify him;
   stand in awe of him,
   all you offspring of Israel!
For he did not despise or abhor
   the affliction of the afflicted;
He did not hide his face from me,
   but heard when I cried out to him.

Psalm 22

Sometimes God appears to withdraw from us;
we feel abandoned, suffering in solitude:
but he is always with us,
ever close, ever vigilant.

MYSTERY OF LIFE

"MASTER, life has dealt bitterly with our hopes and our desires. Our hearts are troubled, and we do not understand. I pray you, comfort us, and open to us the meanings of our sorrows."

And his heart was moved with compassion, and he said: "Life is older than all things living; even as beauty was wingèd ere the beautiful was born on earth, and even as truth was truth ere it was uttered.

"Life sings in our silences, and dreams in our slumber. Even when we are beaten and low, life is enthroned and high. And when we weep, Life smiles upon the day, and is free even when we drag our chains. Oftentimes we call Life bitter names, but only when we ourselves are bitter and dark. And we deem her empty and unprofitable, but only when the soul goes wandering in desolate places, and the heart is drunken with overmindfulness of self.

"Life is deep and high and distant; and though only your vast vision can reach only her feet, yet she is near; and though only the breath of your breath reaches her heart, the shadow of your shadow crosses her face, and the echo of your faintest cry becomes a spring and an autumn in her breast.

"And Life is veiled and hidden, even as your greater self is hidden and veiled. Yet when Life speaks, all the winds become words; and when she speaks again, the smiles upon your lips and the tears in your eyes turn also into words. When she sings, the deaf hear and are held; and when she comes walking, the sightless behold her and are amazed and follow her in wonder and astonishment."

Kahlil Gibran, *The Garden of the Prophet*

> *Profound and mysterious*
> *are the ways of Life;*
> *we cannot comprehend all of Life,*
> *but live with confidence in her.*

THE STILLNESS OF THE SOUL

EVERY soul needs to withdraw from the world from time to time to find the peace which passes all understanding. Every soul needs to be stabilised, and it can only come about in peace and stillness. Once that inner stability has been established, you can go anywhere and do anything without outer chaos and confusion affecting you in any way. Do you enjoy being still, or are you uncomfortable in the stillness? Does it make you squirm to find yourself in the silence, and do you long for noise and action all around you? Do you always want to be busy doing things, and find great difficulty in stilling your body and mind? There are millions of souls in the world who cannot bear silence; they have to have constant noise and action around them. They are restless within and without. I tell you, times of peace and stillness are very precious in a world of turmoil. Seek them, find them and remain in them.

Eileen Caddy, *Opening Doors Within* (29 February)

> *In calm and silence*
> *the soul finds its sustenance;*
> *only thus can the soul hear*
> *and speak to the divinity within.*

BEYOND THE DARKNESS

LIFT your heart to the Lord, with a gentle stirring of love desiring him for his own sake and not for his gifts. Centre all your attention and desire on him and let this be the sole concern of your mind and heart. Do all in your power to forget everything else, keeping your thoughts and desires free from involvement with any of God's creatures or their affairs whether in general or in particular. Perhaps this will seem like an irresponsible attitude, but I tell you, let them all be; pay no attention to them.

What I am describing here is the contemplative work of the spirit. It is this which gives God the greatest delight. For when you fix your love on him, forgetting all else, the saints and angels rejoice and hasten to assist you in every way.

When God's grace arouses you to enthusiasm, it becomes the lightest sort of work there is and one most willingly done. Without his grace, however, it is very difficult and almost, I should say, quite beyond you.

And so diligently persevere until you feel joy in it. For in the beginning it is usual to feel nothing but a kind of darkness about your mind, or as it were, a *cloud of unknowing*. You will seem to know nothing and to feel nothing except a naked intent toward God in the depths of your being. Try as you might, this darkness and this cloud will remain between you and your God. You will feel frustrated, for your mind will be unable to grasp him, and your heart will not relish the delight of his love. But learn to be at home in this darkness. Return to it as often as you can, letting your spirit cry out to him whom you love. For if, in this life, you hope to feel and see God as he is in himself it must be within this darkness and this cloud. But if you strive to fix your love on him forgetting all else, which is the work of contemplation I have urged you to begin, I am confident that God in his goodness will bring you to a deep experience of himself. [...]

When I speak of darkness, I mean the absence of knowledge. If you are unable to understand something or if you have forgotten it, are you not in the dark as regards this thing? You cannot see it with your mind's eye. Well, in the same way, I have not said "cloud", but *cloud of unknowing*. For it is a darkness of unknowing that lies between you and your God.

If you wish to enter into this cloud, to be at home in it, and to take up the contemplative work of love as I urge you to, there is something else you must do. Just as the *cloud of unknowing* lies above you, between you and your God, so you must fashion a *cloud of forgetting* beneath you, between you and every created thing. The *cloud of unknowing* will perhaps leave you with the feeling that you are far from God. But no, if it is authentic, only the absence of a *cloud of forgetting* keeps you from him now. Every time I say "all creatures", I refer not only to every created thing but also to all their circumstances and activities. I make no exception. You are to concern yourself with no creature whether material or spiritual nor with their situation and doings whether good or ill. To put it briefly, during this work you must abandon them all beneath the *cloud of forgetting*. [...]

Now you say, "How shall I proceed to think of God as he is in himself?" To this I can only reply, "I do not know."

With this question you bring me into the very darkness and *cloud of unknowing* that I want you to enter. A man may know completely and ponder thoroughly every created thing and its works, yes, and God's works too, but not God himself. Thought cannot comprehend God. And so, I prefer to abandon all I can know, choosing rather to love him whom I cannot know. Though we cannot know him we can love him. By love he may be touched and embraced, never by thought. Of course, we do well at times to ponder God's majesty or kindness for the insight these meditations may bring. But in the real contemplative work you must set all this aside and cover it over with a *cloud of forgetting*. Then let your loving desire, gracious and devout, step bravely and joyfully beyond it and reach out to pierce the darkness above. Yes, beat upon that thick *cloud of unknowing* with the dart of your loving desire and do not cease come what may.

The Cloud of Unknowing, III-VI

> *Above, a cloud of unknowing;*
> *below, a cloud of forgetting:*
> *solitary and naked, the soul*
> *seeks God by faith and love alone.*

BRAHMAN IS SOUND AND SILENCE

THERE is something beyond our mind which abides in silence within our mind. It is the supreme mystery beyond thought. Let one's mind and one's subtle body rest upon that and not rest on anything else. [...]

There are two ways of contemplation of Brahman: in sound and in silence. By sound we go to silence. The sound of Brahman is OM. With OM we go to the End: the silence of Brahman. The End is immortality, union and peace.

Even as a spider reaches the liberty of space by means of its own thread, the man of contemplation by means of OM reaches freedom.

The sound of Brahman is OM. At the end of OM there is silence. It is the silence of joy. It is the end of the journey where fear and sorrow are no more: steady, motionless, never-falling, ever-lasting, immortal. It is called the omnipresent Vishnu.

In order to reach the highest, consider in adoration the sound and the silence of Brahman. For it has been said: "God is sound and silence. His name is OM. Attain therefore contemplation – contemplation in silence on him." [...]

Even as fire without fuel finds peace in its resting-place, when thoughts become silence the soul finds peace in its own source.

And when a mind which longs for truth finds the peace of its own source, then those false inclinations cease which were the result of former actions done in the delusion of the senses.

Samsara, the transmigration of life, takes place in one's own mind. Let one therefore keep the mind pure, for what a man thinks that he becomes: this is a mystery of eternity.

A quietness of mind overcomes good and evil works, and in quietness the soul is ONE: then one feels the joy of eternity.

If men thought of God as much as they think of the world, who would not attain liberation?

The mind of man is of two kinds, pure and impure: impure when in the bondage of desire, pure when free from desire.

When the mind is silent, beyond weakness or non-concentration, then it can enter into a world which is far beyond the mind: the highest End.

The mind should be kept in the heart as long as it has not reached the highest end. This is wisdom, and this is liberation. Everything else is only words.

Words cannot describe the joy of the soul whose impurities are cleansed in deep contemplation – who is one with his *atman*, his own spirit. Only those who feel this joy know what it is.

Even as the water becomes one with water, fire with fire, and air with air, so the mind becomes one with the infinite Mind and thus attains final freedom.

Mind is indeed the source of bondage and also the source of liberation. To be bound to the things of this world: this is bondage. To be free from them: this is liberation.

Maitri Upanishad, 6

> *In that place in my soul which is silence*
> *is Brahman: the infinite, the eternal;*
> *my true self, the source of*
> *life and joy and liberation.*

LET ME SEE YOUR FACE

AND how shall I invoke my God, my Lord and my God? Since when
I invoke him, I call him into myself: and what place is there in me,
that my God may come into me, God, who made heaven and earth?
Is there indeed, O Lord my God, anything in me which can contain
you? Do heaven and earth, which you have made, and in which you
made me, contain you? Or, because nothing which exists could exist
without you, is it not that everything which exists contains you?
Since I too exist, why do I ask that you enter into me, for I would
not be at all if you were not already in me? For I am not now in hell,
and yet you are there also. For *if I go down into hell, you are there.*
I could not exist, therefore, O my God, I could not be at all, without
your presence in me; or rather, I could not be unless I existed in you,
*of whom are all things, by whom are all things, in whom are all
things.* So it is, O Lord, so it is. Why then do I invoke you, since I
am in you? Or from where can you come to enter into me? Where
can I go beyond heaven and earth, that my God may come there into
me, my God who has said, *I fill the heaven and the earth?* [...]
    What then are you, O my God? What, except the Lord God? *For
who is Lord but the Lord? Or who is God save our God?* O most
high, most good, most powerful, most omnipotent; most merciful
yet most just; most hidden yet most present; most beautiful and most
strong; most constant yet incomprehensible; immutable, yet changing all things; never new, never old, yet renewing all things, and
bringing decay upon the proud, and they do not know it. Always acting and always at rest; always gathering yet lacking nothing;
upholding, filling and protecting; creating, nourishing and perfect-
ing all things; seeking, yet needing nothing.
    You love, but without passion; you are jealous, but without fear;
you repent, but without grief; you are angry, but serene. You change
your works without changing your design; you take back what you
find, yet never lost; you are never in need, yet rejoice in gain. Never
covetous, yet exacting interest: if we give you more than your due,
you become our debtor; but who has anything which does not
belong to you? You pay debts, but owe nothing; forgive debts, but
lose nothing. And what have I now said, O my God, my Life, my
holy Joy? Or what can anyone say when speaking of you? Yet woe

to those who do not speak of you, when even the most eloquent say nothing at all.

Who will grant that I may rest in you? O, who will grant that you would enter into my heart and so inebriate it that I may forget my evil ways and embrace you, my only good? What are you to me? Have mercy on me, that I may say it. And what am I to you, that you should command me to love you, and be angry with me, and threaten me with great misery, if I do not love you? Is it only a slight misery not to love you? O, in the name of all your mercies, tell me, O Lord my God, what you are to me. *Say unto my soul, I am your salvation*: say, that I may hear. See, Lord, the ears of my heart are before you; open them and *Say unto my soul, I am your salvation*. I will run after the sound of this voice and take hold of you. Do not hide your face from me. Let me die, lest I die; only let me see your face.

Saint Augustine, *Confessions*

Who are you, my God,
Heaven and earth cannot contain you,
yet you reside in my heart,
awaiting my love.

OUT OF SILENCE IS BORN THE SOUND

IN the beginning was Silence.
In the Silence within,
Sound was born.
Sound is love.
Sound is the Son of the Divine.
The Divine is Silence.

In the womb of Silence reposed Sound.
Sound became body and was born.
Love is the first radiated image.
THE BODY IS LOVE WHICH HAS BECOME MATTER.

The Divine sets in motion.
Sound is impulse.
Creation is radiated image:
DIVINE LOVE EMBODIED.

The life originated.
From one Sound: Seven[1].
From One: the two halves of life,
Opposition: attraction and repulsion.
From one Sound: Seven;
And from Seven: all forms of life.
Miracle-wonder! Endless stream of Sound.
Creation sings, resounds: divine symphony.
Endless stream of Sound, yet always the Seven.

The two halves of life
     and the seven souls are the key.
The two halves of life
     concentrate and dispense,
     attract and repulse.
Now concentration.
The line of the holy plan is: concentration.

The Divine is: Silence.

---

[1] The seven levels of being: mineral, plant, animal, human, angel, seraph, The Seventh.

The Divine is: Sound.
The Divine is: Harmony.
The Divine is: Love.

Uproar, noise, confusion,
    destructive force which injures the law.
Noise is emptiness,
    and this Ö [the Divine] does not tolerate.
Lips gone silent are not yet Silence.
Sing, my loved ones, sing here below!
Soon the noise will end.
In noise you cannot sing,
    but prepare yourselves: listen!
Above we sing. Listen well! Learn!
Prepare yourselves! Be one with us!
Immeasurable, everlasting love,
    the divine heart is ours.

Cracked pitchers, defective and empty pots and vessels
    are smashed and cast away.
Believe: eternal life is already yours.
That is the noise your ears now hear.
Be new vessels! Golden chalices!
Chalices of transparent gold
    ready to receive divine love!
Chalices in which eternal life can breathe.
Yet even the flawless chalice
    is but radiated image.

The Creator is Silence.
The Son is audible Silence: Sound.

Gitta Mallasz, *Talking With Angels*, 88

> *From the primordial Silence is born*
> *the Sound, harmony and love;*
> *whose opposite is the noise of life without God,*
> *cracked pitchers which are cast away.*

ALL IS VANITY

VANITY of vanities, says the Teacher, vanity of vanities! All is vanity. What do people gain from all the toil at which they toil under the sun? A generation goes, and a generation comes, but the earth remains forever. The sun rises and the sun goes down, and hurries to the place where it rises. The wind blows to the south, and goes around to the north; round and round goes the wind, and on its circuits the wind returns.

All streams run to the sea, but the sea is not full; to the place where the streams flow, there they continue to flow. All things are wearisome; more than one can express; the eye is not satisfied with seeing, or the ear with hearing. What has been is what will be, and what has been done is what will be done; there is nothing new under the sun. Is there a thing of which it is said, "See, this is new"? It has already been, in the ages before us. The people of long ago are not remembered, nor will there be any remembrance of people yet to come by those who come after them. [...]

For everything there is a season, and a time for every matter under heaven:
a time to be born, and a time to die;
a time to plant, and a time to pluck up what is planted;
a time to kill, and a time to heal;
a time to break down, and a time to build up;
a time to weep, and a time to laugh;
a time to mourn, and a time to dance;
a time to throw away stones,
   and a time to gather stones together;
a time to embrace,
   and a time to refrain from embracing;
a time to seek, and a time to lose;
a time to keep, and a time to throw away;
a time to tear, and a time to sew;
a time to keep silence, and a time to speak;
a time to love, and a time to hate;
a time for war, and a time for peace.

What gain have the workers from their toil? I have seen the business that God has given to everyone to be busy with. He has made everything suitable for its time; moreover he has put a sense of past and future into their minds, yet they cannot find out what God has done from the beginning to the end. I know that there is nothing better for them than to be happy and enjoy themselves as long as they live; moreover, it is God's gift that all should eat and drink and take pleasure in their toil. I know that whatever God does endures forever; nothing can be added to it, nor anything taken from it; God has done this, so that all should stand in awe before him. That which is, already has been; that which is to be, already is; and God seeks out what has gone by.

Ecclesiastes, 1 & 3

All that we see is continuously changing;
time flows, flows, flows like the river to the sea;
where is he who does not change,
who is neither created nor destroyed?

8 PATHS TO GOD

THE MANY PATHS

INFINITE *is the numbr of ways leading to the sea of immortality.* It is immaterial *how* you get into this sea. Suppose there is a reservoir of nectar. It is open to you to walk slowly down the sloping bank from *any* point, get to the nectar and have a drink. You get immortal in any case. Again, what does it signify if one throws oneself into the reservoir or is pushed into it by somebody? The result in either case is the same. You taste the nectar – the water of life – in either case. You become immortal. The ways being numberless, *jnana, karma, bhakti,* all lead to God, other things remaining the same.

*   *   *

Do you seek God? Well, seek him in man! His divinity is manifest more in man than in any other object. Look around for a man with a love of God that overflows – a man who yearns for God – a man intoxicated with his love. In such a man has God incarnated himself. God indeed is in all things; only his power is more or less manifest in them. God-incarnate is God's power (divinity) most manifest in the flesh. [...]

The conditioned mind cannot realize God. But he can be realized by the pure mind, which is the same thing as the pure reason, which is the same thing as the pure or unconditioned soul. He cannot indeed be sensed by the finite reason or by the finite, relative, conditioned mind, which has a sensuous nature, and is thus marked by an attachment to "woman and gold" (carnality and worldliness). The mind may get rid of its sensuous nature, be purified by culture, and be once more free from all worldly tendencies, desires and attachments and thus be one with the Unconditioned Soul. Was it not thus that the sages of old saw God? God, the Unconditioned Spirit they saw by means of the purified mind (the mind stripped of its sensuous nature) which they found to be the same as the atman or the Unconditioned Soul within.

* * *

You speak of the path of knowledge or discrimination (*jnana-yoga*). Yes, that path also leads to God. The knowing one says, "One must first be pure if one desires to see God. One must first control one's passions. First self-discipline, then knowledge of God." There is another path leading to God, the path of devotion (*bhakti-yoga*). Once there is in the human soul the love of God, once the chanting of his holy name fills the devotee with joy, no effort is needed for the control of the passions. Such control comes of itself. [...] The living light to which the devotee is drawn does not burn and cause death. It is like the light coming from a gem, shining yet soft, cool and soothing. It does not burn but gives peace and joy.

* * *

I long to worship the Lord in as many ways as I can, and still my heart's desire is not fulfilled! I long to worship him with flowers and fruits and other offerings, to repeat his sacred name by myself, to meditate upon him, to chant his hymns, to dance in the joy of the Lord!

* * *

The Being is the same; only the names are different under different aspects like the substance expressed in different languages as *jal, water, pani, vari and aqua...* God is one, only the names are different. Some call him by the name of *Allah*, some *God*, some *Brahman*, some *Kali*, others again *Rama, Hari, Jesus, Buddha*.

The Gospel of Sri Ramakrishna

> *God is One: but many paths lead to him:*
> *yet the essentials remain the same -*
> *a sincere yearning, purification,*
> *worship and praise.*
> NAKED BEFORE GOD

WHEN you go apart to be alone for prayer, put from your mind everything you have been doing or plan to do. Reject all thoughts, be they good or be they evil. Do not pray with words unless you are really drawn to this; or if you do pray with words, pay no attention to whether they are many or few. Do not weigh them or their meaning. Do not be concerned about what kind of prayers you use, for it is unimportant whether or not they are official liturgical prayers, psalms, hymns, or anthems; whether they are for particular or general intentions; or whether you formulate them interiorly, by thoughts, or express them aloud, in words.

See that nothing remains in your conscious mind save a naked intent stretching out toward God. Leave it stripped of every particular idea *about* God (what he is like in himself or in his works) and keep only the simple awareness *that he is as he is*. Let him be thus, I pray you, and force him not to be otherwise. Search into him no further, but rest in this faith as on solid ground. This awareness, stripped of ideas and deliberately bound and anchored in faith, shall leave your thought and affection in emptiness except for a naked thought and blind feeling of your own being. It will feel as if your whole desire cried out to God and said:

That which I am I offer to you, O Lord, without looking to any quality of your being but only to the fact that you are as you are; this, and nothing more.

Let that quiet darkness be your whole mind and like a mirror to you. For I want your thought of self to be as naked and as simple as your thought of God, so that you may be spiritually united to him without any fragmentation and scattering of your mind. He is your being and in him, you are what you are, not only because he is the cause and being of all that exists, but because he is your cause and the deep centre of your being.

Therefore, in this contemplative work think of your self and of him in the same way: that is, with the simple awareness that he is as he is, and that you are as you are. In this way your thought will not be fragmented or scattered, but unified in him who is all. [...]

Leave your thought quite naked, your affection uninvolved and your self simply as you are, so that grace may touch and nourish you with the experimental knowledge of God as he really is. In this life, this experience will always remain dark and partial so that your longing desire for him may be ever newly kindled. Look up joyfully, then, and say to your Lord, in words or desire:

That which I am, I offer to you, O Lord, for you are it entirely.

Go no further, but rest in this naked, stark, elemental awareness that you are as you are.

The Book of Privy Counselling

> *Let my prayer be thus:*
> *I come before you, my God, as I am;*
> *I wish to be one with you,*
> *as you may be; this, and nothing more.*

THE PATH OF LIGHT

THE INDESTRUCTIBLE, transcendental living entity is called
Brahman, and his eternal nature is called the Self. And action pertaining to the development of these material bodies is called *karma*,
or fruitive activities. The physical nature is known to be endlessly
mutable. The universe is the cosmic form of the Supreme Lord, and
I am that Lord represented as the Supersoul, dwelling in the heart of
every embodied being. Anyone who, at the end of life, quits his
body remembering me, attains immediately to my nature, and there
is no doubt of this. In whatever condition one quits his present body,
in his next life he will attain to that state of being without fail.
Therefore, Arjuna, you should always think of me, and at the same
time you should continue your prescribed duty and fight. With your
mind and activities always fixed on me, and everything engaged in
me, you will attain to me without doubt. By practising this remembrance without being deviated, thinking of the Supreme Godhead,
one is sure to achieve the planet of the divine, the Supreme
Personality, O son of Kunti. Think of the Supreme Person as one
who knows everything, who is the oldest, who is the controller, who
is smaller than the smallest, who is the maintainer of everything,
who is beyond any material conception, who is inconceivable, and
who is always a person. He is luminous like the sun, beyond this
material nature, transcendental. [...]
    I shall now explain to you this process for attaining salvation. The
yogic situation is that of detachment from all sensual engagements.
Closing the door of the senses and fixing the mind on the heart and
the air of life on the top of the head, one establishes this situation.
After being situated in this yoga practice and vibrating the sacred
syllable OM, the supreme combination of letters, if one thinks of the
Lord and thus quits his body, he will certainly reach the spiritual
planets. For one who is without deviation in remembering me, I am
easy to obtain, O son of Partha, because of his constant engagement
in devotional service. After attaining me, the great *mahatmas*, yogis
in devotion, never come back to this temporary world, so full of miseries, because they have attained the highest perfection. From the
highest planet in the material world down to the lowest, all are
places of misery where repeated birth and death take place. But one

who attains to my abode, O son of Kunti, never takes birth again. By human calculation, a thousand ages taken together is the duration of Brahma's one day. And such also is the duration of his night. In the day of Brahma all living entities come into being, and when the night falls all is annihilated. Again and again the day comes, and this host of beings is active; and again the night falls, O Partha, and this host is helplessly dissolved.

There is another, eternal nature, which is transcendental to this manifested and nonmanifested matter. It is supreme and is never annihilated. When all in this world is annihilated, that part remains as it is. That supreme status is called unmanifested and infallible, and it is the highest destination. When one goes there, one never returns. That is my supreme abode. The Supreme Personality of Godhead, than whom no one is greater, is attainable by unalloyed devotion, O Arjuna. Although there in his abode, still he is all-pervading, and everything is fixed within him. [...]

There are two ways of passing from this world, one in light and one in darkness. When one passes in light he does not come back, but when one passes in darkness he returns. O Arjuna, the devotees who know these different paths are never bewildered. Therefore, be always fixed in devotion. A person who accepts the path of devotional service is not bereft of any result of studying the Vedas, performing austere sacrifices, giving charity or pursuing philosophical and fruitive activities. And at the end he reaches the supreme abode.

Bhagavad Gita, 8

Supreme knowledge, knowledge of the Lord,
whence liberation from earthly suffering,
comes from fervent devotion
and constant meditation on the divine.

MANY NAMES BUT ONE TRUTH

MAHAMATI said: "If the Tathagatas are unborn, there does not seem to be anything to take hold of – no entity – or is there something that bears another name than 'entity'? And what can that 'something' be?"

The Blessed One replied:

Objects are frequently known by the different names according to different aspects that they present – the god Indra is sometimes known as Shakra and sometimes as Purandara. These different names are sometimes used interchangeably and sometimes they are discriminated, but different objects are not to be imagined because of the different names, nor can they be without individuation. The same can be said of myself as I appear in this world of patience before ignorant people and where I am known by countless trillions of names.

They address me by different names not realising that they are all names of the one Tathagata. Some recognise me as Tathagata, some as the Self-existent One, some as Gautama the Ascetic, some as Buddha. Then there are others who recognise me as Brahma, as Vishnu, as Ishvara; some see me as Sun, as Moon; some as a reincarnation of the ancient sages; some as one of the 'ten powers'; some as Rama, some as Indra, and some as Varuna.

Still there are others who speak of me as the Unborn, as Emptiness, as 'Suchness', as Truth, as Reality, as Ultimate Principle; still there are others who see me as Dharmakaya, as Nirvana, as the Eternal; some speak of me as sameness, as non-duality, as undying, as formless; some think of me as the doctrine of the Buddha-causation, or of Emancipation, or of the Noble Path; and some think of me as Divine Mind and Noble Wisdom.

Thus in this world and in other worlds am I known by these uncounted names, but they all see me as the moon in water. Though they all honour, praise and esteem me, they do not fully understand the meaning and significance of the words they use; not having their own self-realization of Truth they cling to the words of their canonical books, or to what has been told them, or to what they have imagined, and fail to see that the name they are using is only one of the many names of the Tathagata. In their studies they follow the mere words of the text vainly trying to gain the true meaning, instead of having confidence in the one 'text' where self-revealing Truth is revealed, that is, having confidence in the self-realization of Noble Wisdom.

Lankavatara Sutra

> *All names for the Truth refer*
> *to the same eternal, unchanging One:*
> *which cannot be grasped*
> *by words and names alone.*

THE PRAYER OF THE HEART

WITH my eyes shut I gazed in thought, that is, in imagination, upon my heart. I tried to picture it there in the left side of my breast and to listen carefully to its beating. I started doing this several times a day, for half an hour at a time, and at first I felt nothing but a sense of darkness. But little by little after a fairly short time I was able to picture my heart and to note its movement, and further with the help of my breathing I could put into it and draw from it the prayer of Jesus in the manner taught by the saints, Gregory of Sinai, Callistus and Ignatius. When drawing the air in I looked in spirit into my heart and said, "Lord Jesus Christ," and when breathing out again, I said, "Have mercy on me." I did this at first for an hour at a time, then for two hours, then for as long as I could, and in the end almost all day long. [...]

When about three weeks had passed I felt a pain in my heart, and then a most delightful warmth, as well as consolation and peace. This aroused me still more and spurred me on more and more to give great care to the saying of the prayer so that all my thoughts were taken up with it and I felt a very great joy. From this time I began to have from time to time a number of different feelings in my heart and mind. Sometimes my heart would feel as though it were bubbling with joy, such lightness, freedom and consolation were in it. Sometimes I felt a burning love for Jesus Christ and for all God's creatures. Sometimes my eyes brimmed over with tears of thankfulness to God, who was so merciful to me, a wretched sinner. Sometimes my understanding, which had been so stupid before, was given so much light that I could easily grasp and dwell upon matters of which up to now I had not been able even to think at all. Sometimes that sense of a warm gladness in my heart spread throughout my whole being and I was deeply moved as the fact of the presence of God everywhere was brought home to me. Sometimes by calling upon the name of Jesus I was overwhelmed with bliss, and now I knew the meaning of the words "The kingdom of God is within you" (*Luke*, 17).

From having all these and other feelings I noted that interior prayer bears fruit in three ways: in the spirit, in the feelings, and in revelations. In the first, for instance, is the sweetness of the love of

God, inward peace, gladness of mind, purity of thought, and the sweet remembrance of God. In the second, the pleasant warmth of the heart, fullness of delight in all one's limbs, and the joyous "bubbling" in the heart, lightness and courage, the joy of living, power not to feel sickness and sorrow. And in the last, light given to the mind, understanding of holy scripture, knowledge of the speech of created things, freedom from fuss and vanity, knowledge of the joy of inner life, and finally certainty of the nearness of God and of his love for us.

After spending five months in this lonely life of prayer and such happiness as this, I grew so used to the prayer that I went on with it all the time. In the end I felt it going on of its own accord within my mind and in the depths of my heart, without any urging on my part. Not only when I was awake, but even during sleep just the same thing went on. Nothing broke into it and it never stopped even for a single moment, whatever I might be doing. My soul was always giving thanks to God and my heart melted away with unceasing happiness.

The Russian Pilgrim, *The Way of a Pilgrim*

> *The silent invocation of the holy name of God*
> *opens my spirit and my heart*
> *to the divine presence within me,*
> *to the love of God and all his creation.*

MINDFULNESS

THUS have I heard. At one time the Blessed One was living among the Kurus, at Kammasadamma. There the Blessed One addressed the *bhikkus* thus: "Monks," and they replied to him, "Venerable Sir." The Blessed One spoke as follows:

This is the only way, monks, for the purification of beings, for the overcoming of sorrow and lamentation, for the destruction of suffering and grief, for reaching the right path, for the attainment of nirvana, namely the four foundations of mindfulness. What are the four?

Herein a monk lives contemplating the body in the body, ardent, clearly comprehending and mindful, having overcome, in this world, covetousness and grief; he lives contemplating feelings in feelings...; he lives contemplating consciousness in consciousness...; he lives contemplating mental objects in mental objects...

And how does a monk live contemplating the body in the body? Herein, monks, a monk having gone to the forest, to the foot of a tree or to an empty place, sits down, with his legs crossed, keeps his body erect and his mindfulness alert.

Ever mindful he breathes in, and mindful he breathes out. Breathing in a long breath, he knows "I am breathing in a long breath"; breathing out a long breath, he knows "I am breathing out a long breath"; breathing in a short breath, he knows "I am breathing in a short breath"; breathing out a short breath, he knows "I am breathing out a short breath."

"Experiencing thus the whole breath-body, I shall breathe in," thus he trains himself. "Experiencing the whole breath-body, I shall breathe out," thus he trains himself. "Calming the activity of the breath-body, I shall breathe in," thus he trains himself. "Calming the activity of the breath-body, I shall breathe out," thus he trains himself. [...]

And further, monks, a monk knows when he is going "I am going"; he knows when he is standing "I am standing"; he knows when he is sitting "I am sitting"; he knows when he is lying down "I am lying down"; or just as his body is disposed so he knows it. [...]

And further, monks, a monk, in going forward and back, applies clear comprehension; in looking away, he applies clear comprehension; in bending and stretching, he applies clear comprehension; in wearing robes and carrying the bowl, he applies clear comprehension; in eating, drinking, chewing, and savouring, he applies clear comprehension; in attending to calls of nature, he applies clear comprehension; in walking, standing, in sitting, in falling asleep, in waking, in speaking and in keeping silence, he applies clear comprehension.

Thus he lives contemplating the body in the body internally, or he lives contemplating the body in the body externally, or he lives contemplating the body in the body, internally and externally. He lives contemplating origination-factors in the body, or he lives contemplating origination-and-dissolution factors in the body. Or his mindfulness is established with the thought: "The body exists," to the extent necessary just for knowledge and mindfulness, and he lives detached, and clings to naught in the world. Thus also, monks, a monk lives contemplating the body in the body.

Satipatthana Sutta

The spiritual life is every moment
of every day, every action, every thought:
to be mindful of who we are,
what we are doing.

Sacred Words

THE SPIRITUAL BEING

THERE are four lines which Nature has followed in her attempt to open up the inner being – religion, occultism, spiritual thought and an inner spiritual realization and experience: the first three are approaches, the last is the decisive avenue of entry. [...] Spiritual experience has used all the three means as a starting-point, but it has also dispensed with them all, relying on its own pure strength: discouraging occult knowledge and powers as dangerous lures and entangling obstacles, it has sought only the pure truth of the spirit; dispensing with philosophy, it has arrived instead though the heart's fervour or a mystic inward spiritualisation; putting behind it all religious creed, worship and practice and regarding them as an inferior stage or first approach, it has passed on, leaving behind it all these supports, nude of all these trappings, to the sheer contact of the spiritual Reality. All these variations were necessary; the evolutionary endeavour of Nature has experimented on all lines in order to find her true way and her whole way towards the supreme consciousness and the integral knowledge. [...]

None of the three lines of approach can by themselves entirely fulfil the greater and ulterior intention of Nature; they cannot create in mental man the spiritual being, unless and until they open the door to spiritual experience. It is only by an inner realization of what these approaches are seeking after, by an overwhelming experience or by many experiences building up an inner change, by a transmutation of the consciousness, by a liberation of the spirit from its present veil of mind, life and body that there can emerge the spiritual being. That is the final line of the soul's progress towards which the others are pointing and, when it is ready to disengage itself from the preliminary approaches, then the real work has begun and the turning-point of the change is no longer distant. Till then all that the human mental being has reached is a familiarity with the idea of things beyond him, with the possibility of an other-worldly movement, with the ideal of some ethical perfection; he may have made too some contact with greater Powers or Realities which help his mind or heart or life. A change there may be, but not the transmutation of the mental into the spiritual being. [...]

The last or highest emergence is the liberated man who has realized the Self and Spirit within him, entered into the cosmic consciousness, passed into union with the Eternal and, so far as he still accepts life and action, acts by the light and the energy of the power within him working through his human instruments of Nature. The largest formulation of this spiritual change and achievement is the total liberation of soul, mind, heart and action, a casting of them all into the sense of the cosmic self and the divine reality. The spiritual evolution of the individual has then found its way and thrown up its range of Himalayan eminences and its peaks of highest nature. Beyond this height and largeness there opens only the supramental aspect or the incommunicable transcendence.

Sri Aurobindo, *The Life Divine*

---

*The opening to the inner self and to divinity
does not arise from religious practices alone,
nor from spiritual thoughts,
but from the realization of our spiritual nature.*

THE CONDUCT OF THE BODHISATTVA

THE BUDDHA said to them: "There are the exhaustible and inexhaustible dharmas which you should study. What is the exhaustible?
It is the active (mundane) dharma. What is the inexhaustible? It is
the non-active (supramundane). As bodhisattvas, you should not put
an end to the mundane state; nor should you stay in the supramundane state (*nirvana*).

"What is meant by not exhausting the mundane state? It means
not discarding great benevolence; not abandoning great compassion;
developing a profound mind set on the quest of all-knowledge without relaxing even for an instant; indefatigable teaching and convert-
ing living beings; constant practice of the four bodhisattva winning
methods; upholding the right dharma even at the risk of one's body
and life; unwearied planting of all excellent roots; unceasing appli-
cation of expedient devices and dedication; never-ending quest of
the dharma; unsparing preaching of it; diligent worship of all buddhas; hence fearlessness when entering the stream of birth and
death; absence of joy in honour and of sadness in disgrace; refraining from slighting non-practitioners of dharma; respecting practi-
tioners of dharma as if they were buddhas; helping those suffering
from *klesa* [temptation] to develop the right thought; keeping away
from desire and pleasure with no idea of prizing such a high conduct; no preference for one's happiness but joy at that of others;
regarding one's experience in the state of samadhi as similar to that
in a hell; considering one's stay in samsara as similar to a stroll in a
park; giving rise to the thought of being a good teacher of dharma
when meeting those seeking it; giving away all possessions to realize all-knowledge; giving rise to the thought of salvation when seeing those breaking the precepts. [...]

"This is the bodhisattva not exhausting the mundane state.

"What is the bodhisattva not staying in the supramundane state?
It means studying and practising the immaterial but without abiding
in voidness; studying and practising formlessness and inaction but
without abiding in them; studying and practising that which is
beyond causes but without remaining in it; looking into imperma-
nence without discarding the roots of good causation; looking into
suffering in the world without hating birth and death (samsara);

looking into the absence of the ego while continuing to teach all living beings indefatigably; looking into nirvana with no intention of dwelling in it permanently; looking into the relinquishment of nirvana while one's body and mind are set on the practice of all good deeds; looking into the non-existing destinations of all things while the mind is set on practising excellent actions as true destinations; looking into the unborn (the uncreate) while abiding in the illusion of life to shoulder responsibility to save others; looking into passionlessness without cutting off the passion-stream; looking into the state of non-action while carrying out the dharma to teach and convert living beings; looking into nothingness without forgetting about great compassion; looking into the right position (nirvana) without following the habit of staying in it; looking into the unreality of all phenomena which are neither firm nor have an independent nature, and are egoless and formless, but since one's own fundamental vows are not entirely fulfilled, one should not regard merits, serenity and wisdom as unreal and so cease practising them.

"This is the bodhisattva not staying in the non-active state.

"Further, to win merits, a bodhisattva does not stay in the supramundane, and to realize wisdom he does not exhaust the mundane. Because of his great kindness and compassion, he does not remain in the supramundane, and in order to fulfil all his vows, he does not exhaust the mundane. To gather the dharma medicines he does not stay in the supramundane, and to administer remedies he does not exhaust the mundane. Since he knows the illness of all living beings he does not stay in the supramundane, and since he wants to cure their illnesses, he does not exhaust the mundane.

"Virtuous ones, a bodhisattva practising this dharma neither exhausts the mundane nor stays in the supramundane. This is called the exhaustible and inexhaustible dharma doors to liberation which you should study."

Vimalakirti Nirdesa Sutra, XI

> *The saintly person meditates*
> *on the eternal and the true, but does not*
> *thereby abandon service to others*
> *in the world of impermanence.*

PRAY WITHOUT CEASING (*1 Thessalonians*, 5)

PRAYER is a continual intercourse of the spirit with God. What state of soul is then required that the spirit might thus strain after its Master without wavering, living constantly with him without intermediary?

If Moses, when he attempted to draw near the burning bush, was prohibited until he should remove the shoes from his feet, how should you not free yourself of every thought that is coloured by passion, seeing that you wish to see the One who is beyond thought and perception?

Pray first for the gift of tears so that by means of sorrow you may soften your native rudeness. Then having confessed your sins to the Lord you will obtain pardon for them.

Stand resolute, fully intent on your prayer. Pay no heed to the concerns and thoughts that might arise the while. They do nothing better than disturb and upset you so as to dissolve the fixity of your purpose.

When the devils see that you are really fervent in your prayer they suggest certain matters to your mind, giving you the impression that there are pressing concerns demanding attention. In a little while they stir up your memory of these matters and move your mind to search into them. Then when it meets with failure it becomes saddened and loses heart.

Strive to render your mind deaf and dumb at the time of prayer and then you will be able to pray.

Prayer is the fair flower of meekness and mildness.

Prayer is the fruit of joy and of thanksgiving.

Prayer is the exclusion of sadness and despondency.

Do not pray by outward gestures only, but bend your mind as well to the perception of spiritual prayer with great fear.

At times just as soon as you rise to pray you pray well. At other times, work as you may, you achieve nothing. But this happens so that by seeking still more intently, and then finally reaching the mark, you may possess your prize without fear of loss.

Undistracted prayer is the highest act of the intellect.

Prayer is an ascent of the spirit to God.

Do you long to pray? Renounce all things. You will then become heir to all.

Observe whether you truly stand before God in your prayer or whether you are under some compulsion that drives you to seek recognition from men, striving in this manner after their approval. When indulged to this end your protracted prayer is nothing better than a pretext.

If your spirit still looks around at the time of prayer, then it does not yet pray as a monk. You are no better than a man of affairs engaged in a kind of landscape gardening.

If you are a theologian you truly pray. If you truly pray you are a theologian.

When you are praying do not fancy the Divinity like some image formed within yourself. Avoid also allowing your spirit to be impressed with the seal of some particular shape, but rather, free from all matter, draw near the immaterial Being and you will attain to understanding.

You will not be able to pray purely if you are at all involved with material affairs and agitated with unremitting concerns. For prayer is the rejection of concepts.

Prayer is activity which is appropriate to the dignity of the spirit; or better, it is appropriate for its nobler and adequate operation.

By true prayer a monk becomes another angel, for he ardently longs to see the face of the Father in heaven.

Happy is the spirit which, praying without distraction, goes on increasing its desire for God.

Happy is the spirit that becomes free of all matter and is stripped of all at the time of prayer.

Happy is the spirit that attains to complete unconsciousness of all sensible experience at the time of prayer.

Just as sight is the most worthy of the senses, so also is prayer the most divine of the virtues.

When you give yourself to prayer, rise above every other joy – then you will find true prayer.

Evagrius Ponticus, *Chapters on Prayer*

True prayer is communion
of the spirit with God,
in all purity, without forms,
without earthly attachments.

UNIVERSAL LOVE

HE who is skilled in good and who wishes to attain that state of calm should act thus:

He should be able, upright, perfectly upright, compliant, gentle, and humble. Contented, easily supported, with few duties, of simple livelihood, controlled in senses, discreet, not impudent, he should not be greedily attached to families.

He should not commit any slight wrong such that other wise men might censure him. Then he should cultivate his thoughts thus:

May all beings be happy and secure; may their minds be contented. Whatever living beings there may be – feeble or strong, long, stout, or medium, short, small, or large, seen or unseen, those dwelling far or near, those who are born and those who are yet to be born – may all beings, without exception, be happy-minded!

Let not one deceive another nor despise any person whatever in any place. In anger or ill will let not one wish harm to another. Just as a mother would protect her only child even at the risk of her own life, even so let one cultivate a boundless heart towards all beings.

Let one's thoughts of boundless love pervade the whole world – above, below and across – without any obstruction, without any hatred, without any enmity.

Whether one stands, walks, sits or lies down, as long as one is awake, one should maintain this mindfulness. This, they say, is the sublime state in this life.

Not falling into wrong views, virtuous and endowed with insight, one gives up attachment to sense-desires. Verily such a man does not return to enter a womb again.

Metta Sutta
(Sutta of Benevolent Love)

> *The search for goodness begins with oneself:*
> *may I forever be upright;*
> *may I forever seek the happiness*
> *of all creatures.*

THE WAY OF YOGA

WITH prayers for divine blessings, now begins an exposition of the sacred art of yoga. Yoga is the cessation of movements in the consciousness. Then, the seer dwells in his own true splendour. At other times, the seer identifies with the fluctuating consciousness. [...]

Practice and detachment are the means to still the movements of consciousness. Practice is the steadfast effort to still these fluctuations. Long, uninterrupted, alert practice is the firm foundation for restraining the fluctuations. Renunciation is the practice of detachment from desires. The ultimate renunciation is when one transcends the qualities of nature and perceives the soul. [...]

God is the Supreme Being, totally free from conflicts, unaffected by actions and untouched by cause and effect. God is the unexcelled seed of all knowledge. God is the first, foremost and absolute guru, unconditioned by time. He is represented by the sacred syllable OM, called *pranava*. The mantra OM is to be repeated constantly, with feeling, realizing its full significance.

Meditation on God with the repetition of OM removes obstacles to the mastery of the inner self. These obstacles are disease, inertia, heedlessness, laziness, indiscipline of the senses, erroneous views, lack of perseverance, and backsliding. Sorrow, despair, unsteadiness of the body and irregular breathing further distract the *citta*. Adherence to single-minded effort further prevents these impediments. Through cultivation of friendliness, compassion, joy, and indifference to pleasure and pain, virtue and vice respectively, the consciousness becomes favourably disposed, serene and benevolent. Or, by maintaining the passive state felt at the time of the soft and steady exhalation and during the passive retention after exhalation. Or, by contemplating an object that helps to maintain steadiness of mind and consciousness. Or, inner stability is gained by contemplating a luminous, sorrowless, effulgent light. Or, by contemplating on enlightened sages who are free from desires and attachments, calm and tranquil, or by contemplating divine objects. Or, by recollecting and contemplating the experiences of dream-filled or dreamless sleep during a watchful, waking state. Or, by meditating on any desired object conducive to steadiness of consciousness.

Mastery of contemplation brings the power to extend from the finest particle to the greatest. The yogi realizes that the knower, the instrument of knowing and the known are one, himself, the seer. Like a pure transparent jewel, he reflects an unsullied purity. [...]

When consciousness dwells in wisdom, a truth-bearing state of direct spiritual perception dawns. This truth-bearing knowledge and wisdom is distinct from and beyond the knowledge gleaned from books, testimony, or inference. A new life begins with this truth-bearing light. Previous impressions are left behind and new ones are prevented. When that new light of wisdom is also relinquished, seedless *samadhi* dawns. [...]

Burning zeal in practice, self-study and study of scriptures, and surrender to God are the acts of yoga. The practice of yoga reduces afflictions and leads to *samadhi*. The five afflictions which disturb the equilibrium of consciousness are: ignorance or lack of wisdom, ego, pride of the ego or the sense of "I", attachment to pleasure, aversion to pain, fear of death and clinging to life. Lack of true knowledge is the source of all pains and sorrows, whether dormant, attenuated, interrupted or fully active. [...]

By dedicated practice of the various aspects of yoga, impurities are destroyed: the crown of wisdom radiates in glory. Moral injunctions (*yama*), fixed observances (*niyama*), posture (*asana*), regulation of the breath (*pranayama*), internalization of the senses towards their source (*pratyahara*), concentration (*dharana*), meditation (*dhyana*), and absorption of consciousness in the self (*samadhi*), are the eight elements of yoga.

Non-violence, truth, abstention from stealing, continence, and absence of greed for possessions beyond one's need are the five pillars of *yama*. *Yamas* are the great, mighty, universal vows, unconditioned by place, time and class. Cleanliness, contentment, religious zeal, self-study and surrender of the self to the Supreme Self or God are the *niyamas*. Principles which may run contrary to *yama* and *niyama* are to be countered with the knowledge of discrimination. Uncertain knowledge, giving rise to violence, whether done directly or indirectly, or condoned, is caused by greed, anger or delusion in mild, moderate or intense degree. It results in endless pain and ignorance. Through introspection comes the end of pain and ignorance.

When non-violence in speech, thought and action is established, one's aggressive nature is relinquished and others abandon hostility in one's presence. When the *sadhaka* is firmly established in the practice of truth, his words become so potent that whatever he says comes to realization. When abstention from stealing is firmly established, precious jewels come. When the *sadhaka* is firmly established in continence, knowledge, vigour, valour and energy flow to him. Knowledge of past and future lives unfolds when one is free from greed for possessions. Cleanliness of body and mind develop disinterest in contact with others for self-gratification. When the body is cleansed, the mind purified and the senses controlled, joyful awareness needed to realize the inner self also comes. From contentment and benevolence of consciousness comes supreme happiness. Self-discipline (*tapas*) burns away impurities and kindles the spark of divinity. Self-study leads towards the realization of God or communion with one's desired deity. Surrender to God brings perfection in *samadhi*.

Patanjali, *Yoga Sutras*

> *Purification of the body, purification of the spirit:*
> *that the body may become an instrument*
> *for the liberation of the spirit:*
> *this is the royal way of yoga.*

EVERYDAY LIFE AS PRACTICE

THE most vital element in the practice of the inner way consists in learning to become open and perceptive to the inward experience of essential being. For it is out of essential being that Divine Being speaks and calls to us.

All day we are summoned by the world, which demands that we recognize and master it. At the same time Divine Being is perpetually calling us inward. The world requires of us our knowledge and skill, whereas Divine Being insists that we lay aside knowledge and skill for the sake of inner growth. The world expects us to be continually doing whereas Divine Being requires us, quite simply, *to allow the right thing to happen*. The world tries to keep us on a never-ending treadmill, so that we may achieve something that we in our blindness consider permanent. Divine Being demands that while remaining in touch with it, we refrain, at the same time, from becoming attached to anything at all – even though, in so refraining, we may fear to lose our hold on ourselves. The world encourages us to talk and to do interminably; Divine Being requires that we become quiet and act without acting. The world forces us to concentrate on security; Divine Being asks only that we risk ourselves again and again. To the extent that we comprehend it, the world does our bidding; Divine Being reveals itself only when we accept the incomprehensible. The power of Divine Being becomes apparent at the moment when we let go of the things that support us in the world. It is only when we are able to relinquish that which makes us rich in the world that we are enriched and transformed by Divine Being.

Practice in daily life has many aspects. It requires that we make a movement towards the centre of our being and such a movement inevitably involves a complete change of direction in the world. Through practice we are led to relinquish the world so that our inner-most being may reveal itself. But once we have experienced this inmost core and awoken to our essential being, we begin to sense essence in all things. And so, in the midst of our life in the world, we become aware of Divine Being everywhere.

When essential being becomes inward knowing, we feel a sudden change in ourselves. Relaxed and free, full of strength and light, we are filled with a new and creative life. Those things that lie heavily upon us grow lighter; problems which have been causing anxiety no longer oppress us; and events that in our ordinary state would plunge us into despair now lose their potency. Where every door seemed closed all are now open. We who in ourselves were poor now feel rich, and in the midst of clamour we feel peaceful and calm. It is as though we were bathed in an invisible light which warms and shines upon us. We sense about us a radiance that shimmers through everything. But just as this radiance can dawn upon us without warning, so can it as suddenly disappear. We have no power to make it happen, nor to retain it once it is there. The most we can do is to learn to become prescient and aware of those attitudes which prepare us for such experiences and also, of course, those which prevent them.

The great lesson to be learned, when we are on the threshold of this process of transformation, is to recognize the vital importance of our inner experience, and to accept and admit to consciousness those moods and impulses through which Greater Being reveals itself. Transformation inescapably concerns not a part but the whole person. The time has come for us to comprehend the full significance of this statement. It means that a man must value himself – just as he does another person – in all his wholeness, depth and unity, in a word, as a subject. Only then will he be able to work rightly at the twofold task of cleansing his inner life and correcting his external attitudes. When we have understood that body and psyche are not two separate entities but merely two aspects of the whole way in which a person manifests himself, outwardly and inwardly, we come to understand that work on our inner being will inevitably affect the body, and that efforts to change the body will equally inevitably have their effect within.

Karlfried Graf Dürckheim, *The Way of Transformation*

*In the midst of the clamour of the world,
Divine Being calls us inward,
and asks us to manifest
our essential being in everyday life.*

PRAYER OF THE DEAD
IN THE INTERMEDIATE STATE (THE BARDO)

WHEN through strong unconscious tendencies
I wander in the samsara,
In the luminosity of abandoning all fear,
May the Blessed Ones, peaceful and wrathful,
Go before me,
The wrathful goddesses, Queens of Space,
Behind me;
Help me to cross the bardo's dangerous pathway,
And bring me to the perfect Buddha state.

When parted from beloved friends,
Wandering alone,
My own projections' forms appear,
May the Buddhas send out the power of their compassion
So that the bardo's terrors do not come.

When the five luminous lights of wisdom shine,
Fearlessly may I recognise myself;
When the forms of the peaceful and wrathful ones appear,
Fearlessly and confident
May I recognise the bardo.

When I suffer through the power of evil karma,
May my *yidam* [personal deity] clear away all suffering;
When the sound of the *dharmata* [essence of reality]
Roars like a thousand thunders,
May it become the sound of the six syllables:

[OM MANI PADME HUM].

When I follow my karma, without a refuge,
May the Lord of Great Compassion
Be my refuge;
When I suffer the karma of unconscious tendencies,
May the samadhi of bliss and luminosity arise.

May the five elements not rise up as enemies,
May I see the realms of the five Buddhas.

Bardo-Thödal
(*Tibetan Book of the Dead*)

> *Death is not the final end,*
> *but the passage of the spirit to another life,*
> *where the clear light of the eternal truths*
> *shines without the obscurity of this world.*

THE WAY, THE TRUTH AND THE LIFE

DO not let your hearts be troubled. Believe in God, believe also in me. In my Father's house there are many dwelling places. If it were not so, would I have told you that I go to prepare a place for you? And if I go and prepare a place for you, I will come again and will take you to myself, so that where I am, there you may be also. And you know the way to the place where I am going. [...]

I am the way, and the truth, and the life. No one comes to the Father except through me. If you know me, you will know my Father also. From now on you do know him and have seen him. [...] Whoever has seen me has seen the Father. How can you say, "Show us the Father"? Do you not believe that I am in the Father and the Father is in me? The words that I say to you I do not speak on my own; but the Father who dwells in me does his works. Believe me that I am in the Father and the Father is in me; but if you do not, then believe me because of the works themselves. Very truly, I tell you, the one who believes in me will also do the works that I do and, in fact, will do greater works than these, because I am going to the Father. I will do whatever you ask in my name, so that the Father may be glorified in the Son. If in my name you ask me for anything, I will do it.

If you love me, you will keep my commandments. And I will ask the Father, and he will give you another Advocate, to be with you forever. This is the Spirit of truth, whom the world cannot receive, because it neither sees him nor knows him. You know him, because he abides with you, and he will be in you.

I will not leave you orphaned; I am coming to you. In a little while the world will no longer see me, but you will see me; because I live, you also will live. On that day you will know that I am in my Father, and you in me, and I in you. They who have my commandments and keep them are those who love me; and those who love me will be loved by my Father, and I will love them and reveal myself to them. [...]

The Advocate, the Holy Spirit, whom the Father will send in my name, will teach you everything, and remind you of all that I have said to you. Peace I leave with you; my peace I give to you.

The Gospel According to John, 14

> *The Way, the Truth and the Life:*
> *as I am in the Father and the Father in me,*
> *you are in me and I am in you;*
> *we are ONE in truth and in love.*

LIVE IN THE SPIRIT

WHAT we are is the result of our thoughts. Our nature is shaped by our thoughts and is made up of our thoughts. If a man speaks or acts with an evil thought, suffering follows him as the wheel of a cart follows the foot of the ox that draws the carriage. What we are is the result of our thoughts. Our nature is shaped by our thoughts and is made up of our thoughts. If a man speaks or acts with a pure thought, happiness follows him like a shadow that never leaves him.

"He abused me, he beat me, he defeated me, he robbed me": those who harbour such thoughts will never be free from hate. "He abused me, he beat me, he defeated me, he robbed me": those who do not harbour such thoughts will be free from hate.

For hate never ceases by hate, but hate ceases by love; this is the ancient law. Many do not realize that we all come to an end here, but those who realize it cease their quarrels at once.

He who lives for pleasure only, uncontrolled in his senses, immoderate in his eating, indolent and weak, him Mara, the Tempter, will surely overthrow, as the wind blows down a weak tree. He who lives not for pleasure, his senses controlled, moderate in his eating, faithful and strong, him Mara will not overthrow, any more than the wind blows down a rocky mountain.

He who wishes to put on the yellow robe without having cleansed himself from impurity, who disregards truth and self-control, he is unworthy of the yellow robe. But he who has cleansed himself from impurity, is strong in virtue, temperate and truthful, he is indeed worthy of the yellow robe.

Those who imagine truth to be untruth, and untruth, truth, never arrive at truth, but follow vain desires. But those who know truth to be truth, and untruth, untruth, arrive at truth, and follow right desires.

As rain breaks through an ill-thatched house, passion will break through an unreflecting mind. As rain does not break through a well-thatched house, passion will not break though a reflecting mind.

The evil-doer suffers in this world, and he suffers in the next; he suffers in both. He mourns and suffers when he sees the evil of his own actions. The virtuous man is happy in this world, and he is happy in the next; he is happy in both. He is happy and rejoices when he sees the purity of his actions. [...]

The thoughtless man, even if he recites many scriptures, but does not act according to scripture, does not partake of the spiritual life, but is like a cowherd counting another's cows. The man who follows scripture, even if he can recite but little scripture, having forsaken passion, hatred and delusion, possesses true wisdom and serenity of mind, desiring nothing in this world or that to come, in truth he partakes of the spiritual life.

Dhammapada, 1

Knowledge and practices alone
are not the spiritual life,
but wisdom and love
and a pure and just life.

THE RELIGIOUS MIND

THE RELIGIOUS mind is something entirely different from the mind that believes in religion. You cannot be religious and yet be a Hindu, a Muslim, a Christian, a Buddhist. A religious mind does not seek at all, it cannot experiment with truth. Truth is not something dictated by your pleasure or pain, or by your conditioning as a Hindu or whatever religion you belong to. The religious mind is a state of mind in which there is no fear and therefore no belief whatsoever but only *what is – what actually is.*

In the religious mind there is that state of silence...which is not produced by thought but is the outcome of awareness, which is meditation when the meditator is entirely absent. In that silence there is a state of energy in which there is no conflict. Energy is action and movement. All action is movement and all action is energy. All desire is energy. All feeling is energy. All thought is energy. All living is energy. All life is energy. If that energy is allowed to flow without any contradiction, without any friction, without any conflict, then that energy is boundless, endless. When there is no friction there are no frontiers to energy. It is friction which gives energy limitations. So, having once seen this, why is it that the human being always brings friction into energy? Why does he create friction in this movement which we call life? Is pure energy, energy without limitation, just an idea to him? Does it have no reality? We need energy not only to bring about a total revolution in ourselves but also in order to investigate, to look, to act. [...]

That state of mind which is no longer capable of striving is the true religious mind, and in that state of mind you may come upon this thing called truth or reality or bliss or God or beauty or love. This thing cannot be invited. Please understand that very simple fact. It cannot be invited, it cannot be sought after, because the mind is too silly, too small, your emotions are too shoddy, your way of life too confused for that enormity, that immense something, to be invited into your little house, your little corner of living which has been trampled and spat upon. You cannot invite it. To invite it you must know it and you cannot know it. It doesn't matter who says it, the moment he says "I know", he does not know. The moment you say you have found it, you have not found it. If you say you have experienced it, you have never experienced it. [...]

One asks oneself then whether it is possible to come upon this thing without inviting, without waiting, without seeking or exploring – just for it to happen like a cool breeze that comes in when you leave the window open? You cannot invite the wind but you must leave the window open.

Jiddu Krishnamurti, *Freedom From the Known*

The religious spirit is found in silence,
silence where truth is,
which can enter the soul
only if the window is open.

RELIGION AND LIFE

IS not religion all deeds and all reflection, and that which is neither deed nor reflection, but a wonder and a surprise ever springing in the soul, even while the hands hew the stone or tend the loom?

Who can separate his faith from his actions, or his belief from his occupations? Who can spread his hours before him, saying, "This for God and this for myself; this for my soul and this other for my body?" All your hours are wings that beat through space from self to self.

He who wears his morality but as his best garment were better naked. The wind and the sun will tear no holes in his skin. And he who defines his conduct by ethics imprisons his song-bird in a cage. The freest song comes not through bars and wires.

And he to whom worshipping is a window, to open but also to shut, has not yet visited the house of his soul whose windows are from dawn to dawn.

Your daily life is your temple and your religion. Whenever you enter into it, take with you your all. Take the plough and the forge and the mallet and the lute, the things you have fashioned in necessity or for delight.

For in reverie you cannot rise above your achievements nor fall lower than your failures. And take with you all men: for in adoration you cannot fly higher than their hopes nor humble yourself lower than their despair.

And if you would know God, be not therefore a solver of riddles. Rather look about you and you shall see him playing with your children. And look into space; you shall see him walking in the cloud, outstretching his arms in the lightning and descending in rain. You shall see him smiling in flowers, then rising and waving his hands in trees.

Kahlil Gibran, *The Prophet*

> *Religion permeates life :*
> *all life is religion;*
> *religion is all life.*

IN UTMOST STILLNESS

ATTAIN the utmost stillness;
Maintain perfect quietness.
All things come to be
And thence I see their return.

All creatures flourish,
Then each goes back to its origin.
This return is called tranquillity;
It is the return to destiny.
To return to destiny is called the eternal;
To know the eternal is called enlightenment.
Not to know the eternal is to stumble blindly into disaster.

He who knows the eternal is all-embracing;
Being all-embracing, he is magnanimous;
Being magnanimous, he is royal;
Being royal, he is celestial;
Being celestial, he is in the Tao.
He who attains the Tao is everlasting;
To the end of his days, he is free from danger.

Lao Tzu, *Tao Te Ching*, XVI

In stillness we know the Way:
the Way of all beings,
the return to the origin.

9 PRAYERS AND CELEBRATIONS

THE LORD'S PRAYER

OUR Father who art in heaven,
Hallowed be thy name,
Thy kingdom come,
Thy will be done on earth,
    as it is in heaven.
Give us this day our daily bread,
And forgive us our debts,
    as we forgive our debtors.
And lead us not into temptation,
But deliver us from evil:
[For thine is the kingdom, and the power,
    and the glory, for ever and ever.]

Amen.

The Gospel According to Matthew, 6

> *To pray is to acknowledge God's greatness,*
> *to be humble before him,*
> *to seek the moral and spiritual gifts*
> *we need to serve him.*

THE SATCHITANANDA

O ADORABLE Lord of mercy and love,
Salutations and prostrations unto thee.
Thou art omnipresent, omnipotent and omniscient;
Thou art *Satchitananda.*
Thou art Existence, Knowledge and Bliss Absolute;
Thou art the indweller of all beings.
Grant us an understanding heart, equal vision,
    balanced mind, faith, devotion and wisdom.
Grant us inner spiritual strength to resist
    temptation and to control the mind.
Free us from egoism, lust,
    anger, greed, hatred and jealousy.
Fill our hearts with divine virtues.
Let us behold thee in all these names and forms;
Let us serve thee in all these names and forms.
Let us ever remember thee,
Let us ever sing thy glories,
Let thy name be ever on our lips,
Let us abide in thee for ever and ever.

Swami Sivananda, "The Universal Prayer"

I adore you, Lord of mercy and love,
you who are perfect existence,
knowledge and beatitude:
fill my heart with your divine virtues.

THE BEAUTIFUL NAMES OF GOD

THE MERCIFUL ONE
The Compassionate
The King
The Holy One
The Peace
The Faithful
The Overseer
The Mighty
The Almighty
The Justly Proud
The Creator
The Maker
The Fashioner
The Pardoner
The Overcomer
The Bestower
The Provider
The Opener
He who knows
The Restrainer
The Extender
The Humbler
The Exalter
The Empowerer
The Abaser
The Hearer
He who sees
The Judge
The Just
The Kindly One
The Well-Informed
The Forbearing
The Great One
The Forgiving
The Grateful
The High One

He who is Great
The Guardian
The Nourisher
The Reckoner
The Majestic
The Generous
The Watcher
He who answers
The Comprehensive
The Wise
The Loving One
The Glorious
The Raiser (of the dead)
The Witness
The Truth
The Advocate
He who is strong
He who is firm
The Patron
The Praiseworthy
The Numberer
The Commencer
The Restorer
The Life-Giver
The Death-Giver
The Living One
The Self-Subsistent
The Sublime
The One
The Eternal
The Powerful
He who is able
The Advancer
The Retarder
The First
The Last

The Discoverer
The Evident
The Hidden
The Governor
The Exalted
The Beneficent
The Forgiver
The Avenger
He who pardons
The Kindly One
Ruler of the Kingdom
Lord of Majesty and
 Generosity
The Equitable

The Gatherer
The Rich One
The Enricher
The Giver
The Defender
The Distressed
The Advantager
The Light
The Guide
The Incomparable
He who abides
The Inheritor
The Director
The Long-Suffering

A Litany of the Beautiful
Names of Allah

Innumerable are the names of God
by which he may be addressed,
praised, and loved.

THE THREEFOLD REFUGE

I TAKE refuge in the Buddha;
I take refuge in the Dharma;
I take refuge in the Sangha.
I take refuge in the Buddha, the incomparably honoured one;
I take refuge in the Dharma, honourable for its purity;
I take refuge in the Sangha, honourable for its harmonious life.
I have finished taking refuge in the Buddha;
I have finished taking refuge in the Dharma;
I have finished taking refuge in the Sangha.

THE FOUR GREAT VOWS

However innumerable beings are, I vow to save them;
However inexhaustible the passions are, I vow to extinguish them;
However immeasurable the Dharmas are, I vow to master them;
However incomparable the Buddha-truth is, I vow to attain it.

THE WORSHIPPING OF THE SARIRA

We prostrate ourselves in all humbleness before the holy Sarira representing the body of Sakyamuni, the Tathagata, who is perfectly endowed with all the virtues, who has the Dharmakaya [the real Buddha nature] as the ground of his being, and Dharmadhatu [the Law] as the stupa dedicated to him. To him we pay our respect with due deference. Manifesting himself in a bodily form for our sakes, the Buddha enters into us and makes us enter into him. His power being added to us, we attain enlightenment; and again, dependent on the Buddha's miraculous power, all beings are benefited, become desirous for enlightenment, discipline themselves in the life of the bodhisattva, and equally enter into perfect quietude where prevails infinite wisdom of absolute identity. We now prostrate ourselves before him.

THE TEACHING OF THE SEVEN BUDDHAS

Not to commit evils,
But to do all that is good,
And to keep one's thought pure -
This is the teaching of all the Buddhas.

THE GATHA [CHANT] OF IMPERMANENCE

All composite things are impermanent,
They are subject to birth and death;
Put an end to birth and death,
And there is blissful tranquillity.

Prayers and Chants
From D.T. Suzuki, *Manual of Zen Buddhism*

---

*May the Buddha, the Dharma
and the community of faithful
assist me, together with all beings,
to attain to supreme truth and illumination.*

DEVOTIONAL SONGS OF THE ASHRAM

EARLY in the morning I call to mind that Being which is felt in the heart, which is *sat* (the eternal), *chit* (knowledge) and *sukham* (bliss), which is the state reached by perfect men and which is the super-state. I am that immaculate Brahman which ever notes the states of dream, wakefulness and deep sleep, not this body, the compound made of the elements – earth, water, space, light and air.

* * *

Early in the morning I worship him who is beyond the reach of thought and yet by whose grace all speech is possible. I worship him who the Vedas describe as *neti neti* (not this, not this). Him they, the sages, have called the God of gods, the unborn, the unfallen, the source of all.

* * *

In the early morning I bow to him who is beyond darkness, who is like the sun, who is perfect, ancient, called *Purushottama* (the best among men) and in whom through the veil of darkness we fancy the whole universe as appearing, as in darkness we imagine a rope to be a snake.

* * *

May the Goddess Saraswati, the destroyer completely of black ignorance, protect me. She who is white as the *mogra* flower or the moon and a garland of snow, who has worn white robes, whose hands are adorned with the beautiful bamboo of her *veena* (a kind of violin), who is seated on a white lotus and who is always adored by Brahma, Vishnu, Siva and the other gods.

* * *

I bow to thee the *sat*, the cause of the universe, I bow to thee the *chit*, the refuge of the world, I bow to thee the one without a second, the giver of salvation, I bow to thee the Brahman, the all-pervading, the eternal.

I bow to Vishnu, who is peace incarnate, who lies on a snaky bed, from whose navel grows the lotus, who is the supreme lord of the gods, who sustains the universe, who is like unto the sky, who has the colour of the clouds, whose body is blissful, who is the lord of Lakshmi, who has lotus-like eyes, who is knowable by the yogis through meditation, who dispels the wheel of birth and death and who is the sole ruler of all the worlds.

* * *

Thou art the only refuge, thou art the only one to be desired, thou art the sole protector of the universe, thou art self-revealed, thou art the sole creator, preserver and destroyer of the universe, thou alone art supreme, immovable, unchangeable.

* * *

We think of thee, we worship thee, we bow to thee as the witness of this universe, we seek refuge in thee the *sat*, our only support, yet thyself needing none, the ruler, the barque in the midst of this endless birth and death.

* * *

The face of truth is overlaid with a golden lid, O God, remove it so that I may see the true light. [*Isa Upanishad*]

* * *

OM! From untruth lead me unto truth, from darkness lead me unto light, from death lead me unto life everlasting. [*Brihadaranyaka Upanishad*]

Mohandas Gandhi, *Ashram Bhajanavali*

The words and hymns which I offer to you, my God, bear witness to the belief, devotion and hope of my soul in your goodness and love.

THE GLORIFIED OF GOD

AFTER Jesus had spoken these words, he looked up to heaven and said, "Father, the hour has come; glorify your Son, so that the Son may glorify you, since you have given him authority over all people, to give eternal life to all whom you have given him. And this is eternal life, that they may know you, the only true God, and Jesus Christ whom you have sent. I glorified you on earth by finishing the work that you gave me to do. So now, Father, glorify me in your own presence with the glory that I had in your presence before the world existed.

"I have made your name known to those whom you gave me from the world. They were yours, and you gave them to me, and they have kept your word. Now they know that everything you have given me is from you; for the words that you gave to me I have given to them, and they have received them and know in truth that I came from you; and they have believed that you sent me.

"I am asking on their behalf; I am not asking on behalf of the world, but on behalf of those whom you gave me, because they are yours. All mine are yours, and yours are mine; and I have been glorified in them. And now I am no longer to be in the world, but they are in the world, and I am coming to you.

"Holy Father, protect them in your name that you have given me, so that they may be one, as we are one. While I was with them, I protected them in your name that you have given me. I guarded them, and not one of them was lost except the one destined to be lost, so that the scripture might be fulfilled. But now I am coming to you, and I speak these things in the world so that they may have my joy complete in themselves. I have given them your word, and the world has hated them because they do not belong to the world, just as I do not belong to the world.

"I am not asking you to take them out of the world, but I ask you to protect them from the evil one. They do not belong to the world, just as I do not belong to the world. Sanctify them in the truth; your word is truth. As you have sent me into the world, so I have sent them into the world. And for their sakes I sanctify myself, so that they also may be sanctified in truth.

"I ask not only on behalf of these, but also on behalf of those who will believe in me through their word, that they may all be one. As you, Father, are in me and I am in you, may they also be in us, so that the world may believe that you have sent me. The glory that you have given me I have given them, so that they may be one, as we are one, I in them and you in me, that they may become completely one, so that the world may know that you sent me and have loved them even as you have loved me.

"Father, I desire that those also, whom you have given me, may be with me where I am, to see my glory, which you have given me because you loved me before the foundation of the world.

"Righteous Father, the world also does not know you, but I know you; and these know that you have sent me. I made your name known to them, and I will make it known, so that the love with which you have loved me may be in them, and I in them."

The Gospel According to John, 17

---

*God glorified him whom he sent
on earth, Christ Jesus;
thus as Jesus is in God and God in him,
I am in God and God in me.*

ALL PRAISE BE YOURS, MY LORD

MOST high, all-powerful, good Lord,
   all praise be yours, all glory,
   all honour and all blessing.
To you alone, Most High, do they belong.
No mortal lips are worthy
   to pronounce your name.

All praise be yours, my Lord,
   in all your creatures,
   especially Sir Brother Sun
   who brings the day;
   and light you give us through him.
How beautiful he is, how radiant
   in his splendour!
Of you, Most High, he is the token.

All praise be yours, my Lord,
   for Sister Moon and the Stars;
   in the heavens you have made them,
   bright and precious and fair.

All praise be yours, my Lord,
   for Brother Wind and the Air,
   and fair and stormy and every kind of weather
   by which you nourish everything you have made.

All praise be yours, my Lord,
   for Sister Water;
   she is so useful and lowly,
   so precious and pure.

All praise be yours, my Lord,
   for Brother Fire,
   by whom you brighten the night.
How beautiful he is,
   how gay, robust and strong!

All praise be yours, my Lord,
  for Sister Earth, our mother
  who feeds us, rules us and produces
  all sorts of fruit
  and coloured flowers and herbs.

All praise be yours, my Lord,
  for those who forgive one another
  for love of you
  and endure infirmity and tribulation.
Happy are they who endure these
  in peace for by you, Most High,
  they will be crowned.

All praise be yours, my Lord,
  for our Sister Physical Death
  from whose embrace no mortal can escape!
  Woe to those who die in mortal sin!
Happy are those she finds doing your most holy will!
  The second death can do no harm to them.

Praise and bless my Lord
  and give him thanks and serve him
  with great humility.

        Francis of Assisi, "The Canticle of the Creatures"

> *To see in nature, in the entire universe,*
> *the glory and the goodness of God,*
> *and the homage which is paid to him:*
> *this is itself a great blessing of God.*

MANTRAS

OM OM OM

OM MANI PADME HUM
Hail to the jewel in the lotus (Buddhist – Tibetan)

LA ILLA HA ILLA ALLAH
There is no god but Allah (Muslim)

HARE RAMA HARE RAMA RAMA RAMA HARE HARE
HARE KRISHNA HARE KRISHNA KRISHNA KRISHNA HARE HARE
Hail to Lord Rama! Hail to Lord Krishna! (Hindu)

LORD JESUS CHRIST, SON OF GOD, HAVE MERCY ON ME, A SINNER
LORD JESUS CHRIST, HAVE MERCY ON ME, A SINNER
JESUS CHRIST, HAVE MERCY ON ME, A SINNER
JESUS CHRIST, HAVE MERCY ON ME
CHRIST HAVE MERCY (Christian)

TAT TWAM ASI
That thou art (Hindu)

GATE, GATE, PARAGATE, PARASAMGATE, BODHI SVAHA
Beyond, beyond, the great beyond, beyond
that beyond, to thee homage (Buddhist)

OM NAMO BHAGAVATE VASUDEVAYA
Hail to Lord Krishna! (Hindu)

NAMU AMIDA BUTSU
Adoration to the Buddha of Infinite Light (Buddhist – Japanese)

AMARAM HUM, MADURAM HUM
I am blissful, I am immortal (Hindu)

ALLAH AHKBA
God is great (Muslim)

OM SHANTI
Peace (Hindu)

> *OM SHANTI...The resonance of the mantra*
> *produces in me a calm spirit*
> *and harmony with the Eternal.*

PRAYER AND UNITY

LIFE without prayer is empty and meaningless, for it is that communion with the higher part of you which reveals to you the fullness of this glorious life which is your true heritage. Let your prayers be very positive and constructive, and give thanks for what you are about to receive, even before you pray for it. As you pray, feel a oneness, a unity in all life where there is no separation, for all is one. Prayer unites all; it draws all together and creates perfect oneness. Talk to Me and listen to Me. Never waste time in beseeching Me for this, that and the other, for that is not true prayer. To beseech is to create separateness, and I want you to create oneness at all times. We are one. I AM within you; you do not have to search for Me without. I AM always here waiting for you to recognise Me. Recognise our oneness now; I in you, and you in Me.

Eileen Caddy, *Opening Doors Within* (17 January)

To pray is above all
to unite oneself with God:
by words, by listening, by silence.

THE MASS ON THE WORLD

SINCE again, Lord – though this time not in the forests of the Aisne but in the steppes of Asia – I have neither bread, nor wine, nor altar, I will raise myself beyond these symbols, up to the pure majesty of the real itself; I, your priest, will make the whole earth my altar and on it will offer you all the labours and sufferings of the world. Over there, on the horizon, the sun has just touched with light the outermost fringe of the eastern sky. Once again, beneath this moving sheet of fire, the living surface of the earth wakes and trembles, and once again begins its fearful travail. I will place on my paten, O God, the harvest to be won by this renewal of labour. Into my chalice I shall pour all the sap which is to be pressed out this day from the earth's fruits.

My paten and my chalice are the depths of a soul laid widely open to all the forces which in a movement will rise up from every corner of the earth and converge upon the Spirit. Grant me the remembrance and the mystic presence of all those whom the light is now awakening to the new day.

All the things in the world to which this day will bring increase; all those that will diminish; all those too that will die: all of them, Lord, I try to gather into my arms, so as to hold them out to you in offering. This is the material of my sacrifice; the only material you desire.

Once upon a time men took into your temple the first fruits of their harvests, the flower of their flocks. But the offering you really want, the offering you mysteriously need every day to appease your hunger, to slake your thirst is nothing less than the growth of the world borne ever onwards in the stream of universal becoming.

Receive, O Lord, this all-embracing host which your whole creation, moved by your magnetism, offers you at this dawn of a new day. This bread, our toil, is of itself, I know, but an immense fragmentation; this wine, our pain, is no more, I know, than a draught that dissolves. Yet in the very depths of this formless mass you have implanted – and this I am sure of, for I sense it – a desire, irresistible, hallowing, which makes us cry out, believer and unbeliever alike: "Lord, make us *one*."

Pierre Teilhard de Chardin, *Hymn of the Universe*

> *As the whole of creation is*
> *an offering to you, my God,*
> *I offer to you my efforts,*
> *my pains, my joys of this day.*

HYMN TO AGNI

I PRAY to Agni, the household priest who is the god of the sacrifice, the one who chants and invokes and brings most treasure.

Agni earned the prayers of the ancient sages, and of those of the present, too; he will bring the gods here.

Through Agni one may win wealth, and growth from day to day, glorious and most abounding in heroic sons.

Agni, the sacrificial ritual that you encompass on all sides – only that one goes to the gods.

Agni, the priest with the sharp sight of a poet, the true and most brilliant, the god will come with the gods.

Whatever good you wish to do for the one who worships you, Agni, through you, O Angiras, that comes true.

To you, Agni, who shine upon darkness, we come day after day, bringing our thoughts and homage to you, the king over sacrifices, the shining guardian of the Order, growing in your own house.

Be easy for us to reach, like a father to his son. Abide with us, Agni, for our happiness.

Rig Veda, 1.1

O God, you who are fire eternal,
be with us in our prayer
and accept the flame of our offering.

SIMPLE WONDER

DARE I say that wonder is a prayer?
A butterfly in the spring breeze: wonder.
A sunset over the far hills: wonder.
A star-filled night: wonder.
The crash of an ocean wave: wonder.
The gentle touch of a loving hand: wonder.
The smile of a newborn baby: wonder.
Your presence fills all creation
If only I have eyes to see.

Each moment beckons to me: look beyond.
Beyond the visible, to the Invisible;
Beyond the tangible, to the Intangible;
Beyond the created, to the Uncreated;
Beyond time, to Eternity;
Beyond the finite, to the Infinite;

There, in the emptiness of total destitution,
Naked I come before you,
You who made me in your image,
From your goodness and love:
I have nothing, I am nothing,
That is not from you:
What then can I give you,
What is my offering that is worthy of you?

Do I dare offer to you, simple wonder:
That you are, that you are who you are,
That you see me, that you love me,
That you call me unto you.
This is my prayer,
My Lord, my God, My Creator, my All.

Anonymous

> *I contemplate the magnificence*
> *of your love in all things*
> *and offer to you the simple wonder of a child.*

PRAISE THE LORD!

PRAISE the Lord!

Praise God in his sanctuary;
   praise him in his mighty firmament!
Praise him for his mighty deeds,
   praise him according to his surpassing greatness!

Praise him with trumpet sound;
   praise him with lute and harp!
Praise him with tambourine and dance;
   praise him with strings and pipe!

Praise him with clashing cymbals;
   praise him with loud clashing cymbals!
Let everything that breathes praise the Lord!

Praise the Lord!

Psalm 150

*The entire universe is a manifestation
of the glory of God;
may the entire universe praise God
in all his glory!*

GLOSSARY OF BUDDHIST (B), HINDU (H) AND TAOIST (Tt) TERMS

Origins of terms:

J – Japanese
P – Pali
S – Sanskrit
T – Tibetan

Advaita (S) "Non-dualism"; philosophy whose basis is that the Absolute alone is real (H)

Ahimsa (S) Non-violence; absolute respect for the physical integrity of all living beings (H)

Amitabha (S) Buddha of Infinite Light; Lord of the paradise or "pure land" of the West (in T: *dewachen*) (B)

Ananda (S) Supreme joy, beatitude (H)

Arunachala (S) Sacred mountain in the south of India, location of an important temple dedicated to Siva (H)

Atman (S) The true and immortal Self ("soul"); also the Universal Self, identical to Brahman (H)

Avatar (S) Incarnation of divine consciousness on earth (H)

Avalokiteshvara (S) See Chenrezig

Bardo (T) Intermediate state between the death of an individual and his subsequent rebirth (B)

Bhakti (S) Love of God, devotion; submission to a guru and to the ideal selected; *bhakta*: practitioner of *bhakti-yoga* (H)

Bhikshu (S) Mendicant, monk, male member of the Buddhist *sangha* who has received full ordination (in P, *bhikku*) (B)

Bodhi (P, S) Awakening, illumination; state of Buddhahood; in J, *satori*; also the fig-tree beneath which the historic Buddha achieved illumination; *bohicitta*: aspiration to attain enlightenment for the sake of all beings (B); the equivalent term in (H) is *moksha*.

Bodhisattva (S) Awakened or illumined being; those who aspire to Buddhahood but who forgo nirvana until all sentient beings are saved; a practitioner of the Mahayana path (B)

Brahma (S) God as creator in the Hindu Trinity (H)

Brahman (S)	The eternal and immutable Absolute; the supreme and non-dualist Reality of the Vedanta; pure transcendence (H)
Buddha (P, S)	The Awakened One; an enlightened or awakened person who has completely abandoned all obscurities and perfected all positive qualities; the historic Buddha, Sakyamuni; all those who have achieved the highest truth; synonym for the absolute, ultimate reality, the nature of Buddha (B)
Buddhi (S)	Intellect; mind (H)
Chenrezig (T)	Great Bodhisattva, the Lord of Compassion; one of the original disciples of the Buddha (in S: *Avalokiteshvara*) (B)
Chit (S)	Consciousness or absolute being (H)
Citta (S)	Within the psyche, source of all perception and thought; the conceptual and discriminating spirit (B, H)
Dharma (S)	Natural law of the universe (H) Cosmic law governing the universe; doctrine or teaching of Buddha expressing universal truth; rules and norms of ethical behaviour (B) (in P, *dhamma*)
Guna (S)	Fundamental quality; the three modes of primal energy: *sattva* (purity, serenity, light), *radja* (activity or passion), *rattva* (inertia) (H)
Hri (S)	Syllable characteristic of Buddha Amitabha or connected with him (B)
Hum (S)	Untranslatable final resonating syllable of many mantras, which is intended to extend them to infinity (B, H)
Jnana (S)	Knowledge; understanding; wisdom of the mind to achieve knowledge of God; *jnani*:practitioner of *jnana-yoga* (H)
Kalpa (S)	A cosmic aeon of time (B, H)
Karma (S)	Action; effects or consequences of an individual's acts in this or previous lives; linkage of causes and effects in the moral sphere (B, H)
Koan (J)	Phrase or expression ("case") which presents an opening into ultimate truth, characterised by paradox (B)

Ku (J)	Void, vacuity (in Chinese, *mu*; in S, *shunyata*) (B)
Mantra (S)	Syllable, phrase or sacred text, originally in Sanskrit (by extension in any language), the repetition of which (*japa*) becomes a form of meditation (B, H)
Mara (P, S)	Incarnation of death; the passions; a demon (B)
Maya (S)	Cosmic illusion; the world of phenomena, appearances and forms (B, H)
Nirvana (S)	Delivery from the cycle of rebirths (*samsara*); union with the Absolute; felicity resulting from awareness of one's identity with the Absolute and delivery from all attachment to illusions and desires (in P, *nibbana*) (B)
(*Nirvana*)	State of delivery from *samsara* or illumination; dissolution of the individual self in the Brahman; liberation from suffering, death and rebirth (H)
OM (S)	Untranslatable sacred syllable; in H, the Divine All, Brahman, the Supreme; or the three states of consciousness; in B, the infinity, universality, the void (B, H)
Paramita (S)	"That which attains the far shore"; the transcendental; the six major perfections: charity, discipline, patience, effort or energy, concentration, wisdom (B)
Prajna (S)	Intuitive and immediate wisdom, frequently associated with achieving enlightenment; one of the six *paramitas* (in J – *hannya*) (B) Consciousness as the essence of the *atman* (H)
Prakriti (S)	Primary matter of the universe (H)
Prana (S)	Breath of life (H)
Purana (S)	Collections of stories and legends concerning the Hindu Trinity (Brahma, Siva and Vishnu) (H)
Purusha (S)	Original and eternal man; the supreme being or self ("soul") (H)
Raja-yoga (S)	A yoga based on eight stages, culminating in *dhyana* (meditation) and *samadhi* (H)
Ram/Rama (S)	Avatar, seventh incarnation of Vishnu; hero of the epic poem *Ramayana* (H)

Rishi (S)	Prophet, saint or inspired poet; in particular, those to whom the Vedic hymns were revealed (H)
Sadhaka (S)	Person on the spiritual path of truth (H)
Sadhana (S)	Means of perfection; exercises leading to a mastery of one of the yogas (H)
Samadhi (S)	State of higher consciousness; union of the meditator or subject with the object of meditation; state of non-dualist consciousness (B, H)
Samsara (S)	Cycle of births, deaths and rebirths, before delivery or *nirvana* (B, H)
Sat (S)	Absolute and eternal being; existence (H)
Satchitananda (S)	Existence (*sat*), knowledge (*chit*) and felicity (*ananda*); conceptual approximation of Brahman; also *saccidananda* (H)
Satori (J)	Experience of illumination or *nirvana* (B)
Sattva (S)	See *guna*
Shakti (S)	Lit. strength, energy; consort of Siva; the "divine mother"; the dynamic aspect of God (H)
Siva (S)	One of the three persons of the Hindu Trinity, the divine destroyer (H)
Skanda (S)	The five "aggregates" or categories of physical and mental phenomena which constitute personality: sensation, perception, thought, activity, consciousness (B)
Sravaka (S)	He who hears; a disciple (B)
Sutra (S)	Teaching of Buddha, transmitted by his disciples; by extension, the teaching of the Masters (in P, *sutta*) (B)
Tao (C)	The "Way"; the First Principle which encom- passes all things and generates all phenomena; the ineffable Reality which is the origin of the universe and to which all things return; the goal of man is to achieve unity with the Tao, "the Way" (Tt)
Tathagata (P,S)	"He who has reached"; a realised or enlightened being; one of the titles of Buddha Sakyamuni (B)

Te (C)	"Virtue" or "force"; the active principle of the Tao; the norms and qualities which a thing receives from the Tao; the "virtue" of realization of the Tao (Tt)
Upanishad (S)	Texts comprising the last portion of the revealed Hindu sacred writings, the *Vedas*, the basis of the *Vedanta* (H)
Veda (S)	Knowledge, sacred doctrine; the four great collections of Hindu sacred texts which contain this knowledge; *vedanta*: the collection of philosophical speculations which conclude the Vedas (H)
Vishnu (S)	One of the three persons of the Hindu Trinity, the divinity in its aspect as preserver of creation (H)
Yidam (T)	Deity with which the practitioner of Tantric Buddhism (Tibetan) establishes a personal relationship (B)
Yin-Yang (C)	Fundamental and opposite principles of nature, the alternation and interaction of which gave birth to the universe; *yin* reflects the feminine, passive, receptive, obscure and soft; *yang*, the masculine, active, creative, bright and hard. (Tt)
Yoga (S)	Path or practice leading to knowledge of God; means of spiritual development, of which the principal ones are: *bhakti-yoga, jnana-yoga, karma-yoga, raja-yoga*; *yogi/yogin*: a practitioner of yoga (H)

SPIRITUAL TRADITIONS OF THE TEXTS

BIBLIOGRAPHY

Al-Arabi, Ibn, *The Bezels of Wisdom*. Paulist Press: Mahwah, NJ, 1980.

Al-Arabi, Ibn, *The Tarjuman Al-Ashwaq: A Collection of Mystical Odes*. Theosophical Publishing House: London, 1911.

Al-Arabi, Ibn, *The Meccan Illuminations*: For a French version see Ibn Arabi, *Traité d'Amour*. Albin Michel: Paris, 1986.

Attar, Farid al-Din, *The Ilahi-Nama or Book of God*. Manchester University Press: Manchester, 1976.

Augustine (Saint), *Confessions*: Adapted from translations by Sir Tobie Matthew (1620) and Dr E.B. Pusey (1838). See also the translations by R.S. Pine-Coffin and by Rex Warner.

Aurobindo (Sri), *The Life Divine*. Sri Aurobindo Ashram: Pondicherry, 1960.

Bailey, Alice, *The Reappearance of the Christ*. Lucis Trust: New York & London, 1984.

Bardo Thödol: The Tibetan Book of the Dead: The Great Liberation Through Hearing in the Bardo. Shambhala: Boston & London, 1987.

Basil of Caesarea (Saint Basil the Great), *On the Holy Spirit*. St. Vladimir's Seminary Press: Crestwood, NY, 1980.

Bhagavad Gita: A.C. Bhaktivedanta Swami Prabhupada, *Bhagavad-Gita As It Is*. Bhaktivedanta Book Trust: Los Angeles, 1968.

The Bible: New Revised Standard Version Bible. Collins: London, 1989.

The Cloud of Unknowing and the Book of Privy Counselling. Image Books: New York, 1973.

Caddy, Eileen, *The Dawn of Change*. Findhorn Press, Forres, Scotland, 1979.

Caddy, Eileen, *Opening Doors Within*. Findhorn Press, Forres, Scotland, 1987.

Chenrezig Puja. Kagyu Changchub Chuling & Kagyu Droden Kunchab, 1982.

Chögyam Trungpa, *Cutting Through Spiritual Materialism*. Shambhala: Boston & London, 1987.

Chuang Tzu, *The Complete Works of Chuang Tzu*. Columbia University Press: New York, 1968.

A Course in Miracles. Arkana: London, 1985.

Desjardins, Arnaud, *Les Chemins de la Sagesse*. [Vol.I] La Table Ronde: Paris, 1969.

Deshimaru, Taisen, *La Pratique du Zen*. Albin Michel: Paris, 1981.

Deshimaru, Taisen, and Philippe Coupey, *La Voix de la Vallée: L'Enseignement d'un Maître Zen*. Rocher: Paris, 1984.

Dhammacakkappavattana Sutta: in Walpola Rahula, *What the Buddha Taught*. Wisdom Books: London, 1990.

Dhammapada: Adapted from the translation by Max Muller, in *The Sacred Books of the East*, Vol. 10. Oxford University Press, 1881. See also translations by S. Radhakrishnan, Eknath Easwaran and Juan Mascaró.

Dürckheim, Karlfried Graf, *The Way of Transformation: Daily Life as Spiritual Exercise*. George Allen & Unwin: London, 1985.

Eckhart (Meister), *Meister Eckhart: A Modern Translation*. Harper & Row: New York, 1941.

Evagrius Ponticus, *The PraktiKos: Chapters on Prayer*. Cistercian Publications: Spencer, MS, 1972.

Francis of Assisi (Saint), *The Prayers of St Francis*. Darton, Longman and Todd: London, 1988.

Gandhi, Mohandas, *The Collected Works of Mahatma Gandhi*. Vol. XLIV. Ministry of Information and Broadcasting: New Delhi, 1971.

Gibran, Kahlil, *The Prophet*. Arkana: London, 1992.

Gibran, Khalil, *The Garden of the Prophet*. Heinemann: London, 1935.

The Gospel of Thomas: in James M. Robinson, ed., *The Nag Hammadi Library in English*. Harper San Franciso, 1990.

Gregory of Nazianzen, *Selected Poems*. SLG Press: Oxford, 1986.

Hildegard of Bingen, *Book of Divine Works*. Bear: Santa Fe, NM, 1987.

Huang Po in: John Blofeld, *The Zen Teaching of Huang Po: On the Transmission of Mind*. The Buddhist Society: London, 1985.

Huxley, Aldous, "Being" in Christopher Isherwood, ed., *Vedanta for the Western World*. George Allen & Unwin Ltd.: London, 1948.

John Chrysostom (Saint), *On the Incomprehensible Nature of God*. Catholic University of America Press: Washington, DC, 1982.

John of the Cross (Saint), *The Collected Works of St. John of the Cross*. ICS Publications: Washington, DC, 1991.

Kabir: in Rabindranath Tagore, *One Hundred Poems of Kabir*. Macmillan & Co.: London, 1915.

The Koran. Penguin: London, 1990.

Krishnamurti, Jiddu, "The Dissolution of the Order of the Star" (1929), reprinted in *Bulletin*, Krishnamurti Foundation of America, No. 53, 1986.

Krishnamurti, Jiddu, *Freedom From the Known.* Krishnamurti Foundation: Madras, 1992.

Krishnamurti, Jiddu, *Now.* Star Publishing: Eerde, Netherlands [1929].

Lankavatara Sutra: in Dwight Goddard, *A Buddhist Bible.* George G. Harrap & Co.: London, 1956.

Lanza del Vasto, *Principes et Préceptes du Retour à l'Evidence.* Denoël-Gonthier: Paris, 1973.

Lao Tzu, *Tao Te Ching*: Adapted from several English and French translations. See also translations by D.C. Lau (Penguin) and Arthur Waley (George Allen & Unwin).

Law, William, *The Spirit of Prayer and the Spirit of Love.* James Clarke & Co.: Cambridge, 1969.

Le Saux, Henri, *La Montée au Fond du Coeur.* OEIL: Paris, 1986.

Mallasz, Gitta, *Talking With Angels.* Daimon Verlag: Einsiedeln, Switzerland, 1992.

Merton, Thomas, *No Man Is an Island.* Harcourt Brace Jovanovich: New York, 1978.

Merton, Thomas, *New Seeds of Contemplation.* New Directions: New York, 1961.

Merton, Thomas, *The Wisdom of the Desert: Sayings from the Desert Fathers.* Sheldon Press: London, 1974.

Metta Sutta: in Walpola Rahula, *What the Buddha Taught.* Wisdom Books: London, 1990.

Milarepa, *The Hundred Thousand Songs of Milarepa.* Shambhala: Boston & Shaftesbury, 1989.

Mumen Ekai, *Gateless Gate.* Center Publications: Los Angeles, 1979.

Narada: Adapted from several versions. See Swami Tyagrisananda, *Aphorisms on the Gospel of Divine Love.* Sri Ramakrishna Math: Madras, 1978.

Ninety-Nine Most Beautiful Names of Allah: in Arthur Jeffrey, *A Reader on Islam.* Mouton & Co.: The Hague, 1962.

Nityanaimittika-pathavali: in Jaini, P.S., *The Jaina Path of Purification.* University of California Press: Berkeley, CA, 1975.

Patanjali: in B.K.S. Iyengar, *Light on the Yoga Sutras of Patanjali.* Aquarian/Thorsons: London, 1993.

Plotinus, *The Enneads.* Penguin: London, 1991.

Prajnaparamita Sutra: in D.T. Suzuki, *Manual of Zen Buddhism.* Rider: London, 1983.

Pseudo-Dionysius, *The Complete Works.* Paulist Press: Mahwah, NJ, 1987.

Rig Veda: in Wendy Doniger O'Flaherty, trans., *The Rig Veda: An Anthology*. Penguin: London, 1981.

Ramakrishna (Sri): in [Mahendranath Gupta], *The Gospel of Sri Ramakrishna (According to M)*. Ramakrishna Math: Madras, 1930.

Ramana Maharshi, "Sri Arunachala Pancharatna": *The Collected Works of Ramana Maharshi*. Rider: London, 1959.

Ramana Maharshi, "Teachings": Arthur Osborne, ed., *The Teachings of Bhagavan Ramana Maharshi*. Rider: London, 1971.

Rumi, Jalal od-Din, *The Mathnawi of Jalalu'Ddin Rumi*. Vol. VI. Cambridge University Press: Cambridge, 1934.

Rumi, Jalal od-Din, *Selected Poems from the Divani Shamsi Tabriz*. Cambridge University Press: Cambridge, 1952.

Rumi, Jalal od-Din, *The Ruba'iyat of Jalal ad-Din Rumi*. Emery Walker: London, 1949.

Saichi: in D.T. Suzuki, *Mysticism: Christian and Buddhist*. Harper & Brothers: New York, 1957.

Shankaracharya, *Nirvan Sthotra*: See Alexandra David Neel, *Astavakra Gîtâ suivi de l'Avadhuta Gîtâ*. Rocher: Paris, 1979.

Shankaracharya, *Vivekachudamani*: *The Crest-Jewel of Discrimination*. John M. Watkins: London, 1964.

Satipatthana Sutta: in Thich Nhat Hanh, *The Miracle of Mindfulness: A Manual on Meditation*. Rider: London, 1991.

Suzuki, D.T., *Manual of Zen Buddhism*. Rider: London, 1983.

Symeon the New Theologian, *The Discourses*. Paulist Press: Mahwah, NJ, 1980.

Tagore, Rabindranath, *Sadhana: The Realisation of Life*. Macmillan: London, 1916.

Teilhard de Chardin, Pierre, *Hymn of the Universe*. Collins: London, 1965.

Tenzin Gyatso (Dalai Lama), *Kindness, Clarity and Insight*. Snow Lion Publications: Ithaca, NY, 1984.

Teresa of Jesus (Avila) (Saint), *Complete Works*. Sheed and Ward: London, 1991.

Thomas à Kempis, *The Imitation of Christ*: Adapted from the translation by F.B. (Antony Hoskins, 1677), revised by John Worthington (1841). See also the translation by Leo Sherley-Price.

The Thunder: Perfect Mind: in James M. Robinson, ed., *The Nag Hammadi Library in English*. HarperSanFrancisco, 1990.

Tilopa: in Chögyam Trungpa, *The Myth of Freedom and the Way of Meditation*. Shambhala: Boulder, CO & London, 1976.

The Upanishads. Penguin: London, 1965.

The Vimalakirti Nirdesa Sutra. Shambhala: Boston & Shaftesbury, 1990. Vivekananda (Swami), *The Complete Works of Swami Vivekananda.* Vol. III. Advaita Ashrama: Calcutta, 1991.

The Way of a Pilgrim. [The Russian Pilgrim] SPCK: London, 1972.

Yoka Daishi: in D.T. Suzuki, *Manual of Zen Buddhism.* Rider: London, 1983.

COPYRIGHT NOTICES

Introducing Findhorn Press

Findhorn Press is the publishing business of the Findhorn Community which has grown around the Findhorn Foundation, co-founded in 1962 by Peter and Eileen Caddy and Dorothy Maclean. The first book originated from the early interest in Eileen's guidance over 20 years ago and Findhorn Press now publishes not only Eileen Caddy's books of guidance and inspirational material, but many other books, and it has also forged links with a number of like-minded authors and organisations.

For further information about the Findhorn Community and
how to participate in its programmes please write to:
The Accommodation Secretary Findhorn Foundation
Cluny Hill College, Forres IV36 0RD, Scotland
tel. +44 (0)1309-673655 fax +44 (0)1309 673113
e-mail reception@findhorn.org
http://www.mcn.org/findhorn/index.html

For a complete catalogue,
or for more information about Findhorn Press products,
please contact:
Findhorn Press
The Park, Findhorn, Forres IV36 0TZ, Scotland
tel. +44 (0)1309-690582 fax +44 (0)1309 690036
e-mail thierry@findhorn.org
http://www.mcn.org/findhorn/press/ *or*
http://www.gaia.org/findhornpress/

Books by Eileen Caddy (published by Findhorn Press)

OPENING DOORS WITHIN

Eileen Caddy's bestseller – 365 pieces of guidance received during her meditations, one for each day of the year. They contain simple yet practical suggestions, for living life with joy, inspiration and love. Translated into 14 languages, this treasure of a book is the perfect present for loved ones. Now available in both hardcover and paperback.

Hard cover	110x155mm	£10.95	404 pages	ISBN 0 905249 66 6
Paperback	110x155mm	£6.95	404 pages	ISBN 0 905249 68 2

THE LIVING WORD

A pocket-sized book of short meditations given to Eileen in times of silence and used by her over the years for the deepening of her own spiritual life. They are intended for use by those wishing to expand their awareness of the divine and to express it in their lives.

Pbk	150x105mm	£3.95	110 pages	ISBN 0 905249 69 0

GOD SPOKE TO ME

Eileen's first book of guidance received during the early days of the Findhorn Community. Its message affirms the inherent wisdom and intelligence of all life and the ability of each one of us to contact it by turning within.

Pbk	214x135mm	£5.95	142 pages	ISBN 0 905249 81 X

FOOTPRINTS ON THE PATH

A further selection of Eileen's inspirational writings which she offers as an aid to contact with the divine source and a complete teaching in how to live a spiritual life.

Pbk	214x135mm	£5.95	183 pages	ISBN 0 905249 80 1

FOUNDATIONS OF A SPIRITUAL COMMUNITY

Guidance that helped the Caddy family, living in a tiny caravan, become the international spiritual community called Findhorn. The central principal of turning within to find the true source of faith, inspiration and love makes this book relevant not only for those building a spiritual community but also for all who live ordanary lives in our wider society.

Pbk	214x135mm	£5.95	175 pages	ISBN 0 905249 78 X

THE DAWN OF CHANGE

A selection of daily guidance on human problems relating to work, relationships, purpose, health, inner life etc. Eileen tells how all of us may experience "the dawn of change".

Pbk	214x135mm	£5.95	190 pages	ISBN 0 905249 87 9

THE SPIRIT OF FINDHORN

This book offers a brief history of how Eileen gave up everything to follow her inner voice as well as sharing much of the guidance and wisdom which supported Eileen through the early das of her spiritual transformation and the birth of the Findhorn Community.

Pbk	214x135mm	£5.95	142 pages	ISBN 0 905249 97 6